PASTA
From A to Z

A COMET BOOK

A Comet Book
Published in 1986
by the Paperback Divsion of
W.H. Allen & Co. PLC
44 Hill Street, London WIX 8LB

First published in Italy by Gruppo Editoriale Fabbri

Copyright © 1984 by Gruppo Editoriale Fabbri-Bompiani,
Sonzogno, Etas S.p.A., Milan

English language translation copyright © by Gruppo Editoriale
Fabbri S.p.A., Milan, 1986

Translated by Mary Stuttard

Production services by Studio Asterisco, Milan

Printed and bound in Italy
by Gruppo Editoriale Fabbri S.p.A., Milan

ISBN 0-86379-116-6

CONTENTS

GLOSSARY

al dente: this expression is used to describe the degree of "readiness" of cooked pasta, which should be firm, not soft and sticky. The only way to know is by trying it!

ricotta: a fresh, unsalted curd cheese (rather like cottage cheese)

mascarpone: a very rich cream cheese

mozzarella: a fresh, bland, white buffalo's or cow's milk cheese, sold in its own liquid

fontina and bitto: both resemble a smooth gruyère; the first is made from cow's milk in the Aosta Valley, the second is a goat's milk cheese from Valtellina. (Try processed cheese as an alternative.)

pecorino: a hard, mature, sheep's milk cheese, often used in the same way as parmesan cheese

porcini: boletus mushrooms, tastier than cultivated mushrooms; the dried variety is easier to find in the shops and handier to keep in the kitchen, hence their use in various recipes in this book.

salsiccia: a coarse, spicy kind of Italian sausage.

mortadella: or Bologna sausage (the old "polony"); a smooth, steamed sausage you can buy from a delicatessen. Try to avoid the usual British-type sausage, your dishes will taste for more authentic!

HOME-MADE PASTA

Kneading together flour and water was perhaps one of man's first actions looking back through his history. The first bread was simply an unleavened dough made from flour and water; even today, among some primitive peoples, the use of yeast is completely unknown. However, all cultures are familiar with the art of kneading even if they do not all use the same ingredients. These are usually chosen according to what is available locally: basically flours of various cereals mixed with water alone or enriched with eggs and perhaps oil.

Pasta casalinga (home-made pasta), or fresh pasta, now generally implies egg pasta; it contains one egg for every 100 g (3½ oz) flour, making it extremely nutritious. Why not prepare it once in a while? You may rediscover long-forgotten aromas and flavours... helped by modern equipment which greatly reduces the time and effort once involved in its preparation.

Some may object that home-made pasta with its high calory content is a food hardly suitable for the sedentary life of modern man. In fact, a normal plate of pasta contains about 360 calories, most of which are derived from its high carbohydrate and low protein content. Modern nutritional science has recently established that pasta is not fattening if it is properly seasoned and included within a correct and well-balanced diet. Indeed, it is advisable to introduce pasta into the daily diet because wheat flour, especially wholemeal flour, that has been organically grown and not chemically refined, contains mineral salts and many important vitamins from the B, E, F and PP groups.

So pasta made with one egg for every 100 g (3½ oz) flour has a remarkable nutritional value. If soft-grain wheat flour is less protein-rich than that derived from durum wheat, used for making industrial pastas, this deficiency is largely compensated by the nutritious substances contained in the eggs (especially the whites), other proteins of animal origin and a high percentage of fats.

All this combined with its astounding versatility fully justifies the great importance pasta assumes in the Italian diet. Frequently

served with very rich sauces and dressings including a variety of cheeses and often with tasty meat, fish or vegetable fillings, pasta can provide the basis for an infinite quantity of mouthwateringly unforgettable dishes, within everyone's means and ready to satisfy the fussiest and most refined of palates.

HOW TO MAKE PASTA BY HAND

Utensils — The good old-fashioned rolling-pin and a pastry-board are still the tools most used even nowadays for making pasta at home. The board should be fairly large and perfectly smooth. Other basic essentials are a small serrated or smooth cutting-wheel and a scraper or spatula for removing the dough from the board.

Ingredients and quantities — Home-made egg pasta usually needs 1 egg for every 100 g (3½ oz) flour. The quantity of flour for 4 persons depends on how the pasta is destined to be used: 400 g (14 oz) for pastasciutta (served with a plain sauce or dressing), 300 g (10 oz) if you intend to dress it with a rich sauce, 200 g (7 oz) for pasta in brodo (served in broth or soup). It is important to use fresh flour, warm white in colour, soft and sweet smelling. The darker the colour, the less refined the flour. Durum wheat semolina found in healthfood shops gives good results, but for those with no nearby source, plain white and wholemeal flour or semolina will do just as well.

Pasta dough — Pour a mound of flour onto the pastry-board, make a "crater" in the centre and break in the eggs. If you wish, you can beat the eggs in a basin as for an omlette, then pour them into the "crater". You may replace one egg with a shellful of water in order to make a less rich pasta, or you may add a tablespoon of oil to render the dough more elastic. In some cases you may even add a little white wine, but remember, traditional recipes do not allow for these variations.

Add a pinch of salt and begin to incorporate the flour and eggs slowly with your fingertips. Now use your hands to knead the dough for at least 10-15 minutes, re-flouring the pastry-board from time to time and scraping off any dough sticking to it with

a spatula. Work the dough until it is soft, smooth and elastic.
Every so often the dough should be stretched out, folded over and kneaded again.

When air bubbles start to form, gather the dough into a ball, sprinkle it with a handful of flour and leave it to stand on the board for about 15 minutes, covered with a bowl or cloth (see figg. 1-5, pp. 8-9).

Rolling out — Experts may well leave the dough in one piece, but novices are better dividing it into two or four and rolling out one piece at a time.

Begin by pressing out the dough a little with the palms of your hands, then roll it out firmly and evenly with the rolling-pin. Always roll from the centre out in all directions, rotating the dough to make it round and evenly thin.

The thinner and larger it becomes, the more difficult it is to turn. Help yourself by wrapping it round the pin, turning it and replacing it gently on the board. Towards the end wrap it partially around the pin, turn slightly to the left, stretching it out carefully at the same time. Continue this manoevre until the dough reaches the required thinness (see figg. 6-8, p. 9).

An ideal, all-purpose thickness is about 2 mm ($\frac{1}{16}$ inch), varying for certain special types of pasta.

Owners of electric or manual pasta machines may save time and effort for rolling out the dough, but perhaps the result may not be so satisfying, as it will lack the delicately genuine texture of hand-rolled pasta.

1
Heap the flour on the pastry-board, make a "crater" in the centre and break in the eggs.

2
With the tips of your fingers, gradually incorporate the eggs and flour.

3
Mix for 10-15 minutes, scraping the sticky surplus off the board with a spatula.

4
Knead vigorously, using the inner part of the wrists to obtain a soft, evenly-mixed dough.

5
Stretch the dough out occasionally, fold it over again and go on kneading.

6
Press the dough flat with your hands and roll it out firmly with the rolling-pin.

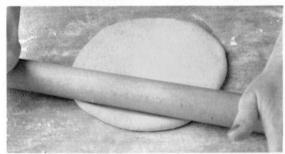

7
Starting from the centre, roll out the dough in all directions, rotating it after each roll, to obtain a circular shape.

8
Now and again, wrap the thinning dough around the rolling-pin, turn it gradually, and pull gently to stretch it.

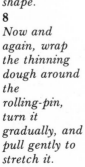
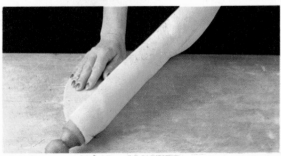

DIFFERENT PASTA SHAPES

When using an electric machine, you can prepare the dough and proceed at once to form the desired pasta shape. If you are using the traditional "rolling-pin and elbow grease" method, after rolling out a thin piece of dough you must let it stand for a few minutes. When cutting dough by hand, bear in mind that you need a heavy knife with a sharp, wide blade or you will risk squashing the pasta instead of cutting it cleanly. Proceed as follows to make the most common pasta shapes.

Tagliatelle or fettucce (ribbons) — Pasta strips about 1 cm (½ inch) wide. Roll up the sheet of dough quite tightly and cut it with a wide-bladed knife into 1 cm (½ inch)-wide strips (see fig. 1, p. 12). Open the small rolls of pasta by hand or by inserting the blunt edge of a knife and lifting them up; alternatively, you may pick up the rolls, a small handful at a time, and drop them onto the board, allowing the coils to open on their own.

Tagliatelle are usually served dry, that is, not in broth, and are excellent even simply dressed with butter or fresh tomato sauce, and parmesan cheese.

Fettuccine or linguine (narrow ribbons or small tongues) — They are strips of pasta, rather like tagliatelle, but a little less than ½ cm (¼ inch) wide. They are mainly served dressed with oil or butter, with or without cheese, with cream, peas and ham, or with béchamel (white sauce).

Tagliatelline or tagliolini or taglierini — These are even narrower strips of pasta 2-3 mm (¹⁄₁₆ to ⅛ inch) wide. Though usually served in meat broth, they are also good with a sauce or dressing and are especially well liked by children.

Quadrettini or quadrucci — Small 1 cm (½ inch) pasta squares. To make them, roll up the pasta as usual and cut it into 1 cm (½ inch)-wide strips; now turn the small rolls of pasta and cut them crosswise, thus obtaining 1 cm (½ inch) squares (see fig. 2, p. 12). To make these squares with a machine, simply chop the strips to the same length as the rollers of your machine and then feed them sideways to the machine, a small group at a time. Pasta squares are mainly served in meat, chicken or vegetable broth.

Maltagliati ("badly cut") — Small pieces of pasta cut irregularly, usually in a diamond shape. After rolling up the dough as described above for tagliatelle, cut it into random strips 1 cm (½ inch) wide along one side. You will obtain small pasta "diamonds", mainly served in broth with vegetables (chick-peas or beans) (see fig. 3, p. 12).

Farfalle, nodini or galani (butterflies, knots or bows) — Small rectangles of pasta pinched in the middle to make the characteristic butterfly form. Before the dough dries too much, cut horizontal strips 1-2 cm (½ inch to 1 inch) wide with the cutting-wheel. The width depends on whether you want to serve the pasta in broth, in which case the pieces should be narrow. Without moving the strips, cut them into 4 cm (2 inch)-wide rectangles. Form the butterflies by pinching the rectangles in the middle (see fig. 4, p. 12). Farfalle etc. can be dressed with tomato sauce, peas and ham, the juices from stews or roast joints, or with cream sauces.

Pappardelle — Long strips of pasta 2-3 cm (1 to 1½ inches) wide, cut with a serrated cutting-wheel from a flat sheet of dough (see fig. 5, p. 12). They are often served with rich, meaty sauces, giblets, game or mushroom sauces.

Lasagne — Strips of pasta at least 8 cm (4 inches) wide, cut with a knife or smooth cutting-wheel into squares or rectangles of the desired size (see fig. 6, p. 12). They are then spread out on a floured board to dry, and are used for oven-baked, layered pasta dishes or for "cannelloni ripieni" (large stuffed pasta rolls).

11

1 Tagliatelle *or* fettucce: *roll up the dough, then cut it into 1 cm (¹/₂ inch)-wide "ribbons".*

2 Quadrettini *or* quadrucci: *cut the flat dough into "ribbons", then across into squares.*

3 Maltagliati: *roll out the dough and cut it obliquely into small irregular diamond shapes.*

4 Farfalle *or* nodini: *make rectangles with a cutting-wheel and pinch in the middle.*

5 Pappardelle: *cut the thin dough lengthwise into 2-3 cm (1 to 1¹/₂ inch)-wide strips.*

6 Lasagne: *using a smooth cutting-wheel or knife cut squares from the sheet of dough.*

STUFFED PASTA

If the pasta is to be stuffed it will have to be softer in order to be rolled thinly. You will find several variations on the basic recipe, such as reducing the number of eggs, adding the appropriate amount of water and in some cases a little olive oil or white wine.

The dough should be used straight away, as soon as it has been rolled out. Distribute the filling on the dough, remembering to cover the area you are not using with a clean cloth to keep it from drying too quickly. Make the stuffed pasta by folding, cutting and sealing the filled dough according to the chosen recipe. Dabbing the edges with beaten egg or egg-white helps damp them should they seem too dry, and pressing lightly with your fingertips seals the pasta and prevents the filling from seeping out during cooking.

DIFFERENT TYPES OF STUFFED PASTA

Agnolini — A speciality of Mantuan cookery, agnolini have spread throughout lower Lombardy and Emilia where, depending on the area, their filling and even their name may vary.
They are usually served either with butter and cheese, with butter cheese and cream, or boiled in broth which in this case must be very refined, for example, the typically Emilian agnolini are cooked in capon and beef broth.
To make agnolini use a pasta cutting-wheel to cut the dough into 4 cm (2 inch) squares; roll the filling into little balls and place one in the centre of each square. Fold the dough over the filling to form a triangle. Seal the dough firmly to prevent the filling from seeping out during cooking. Wrap the triangle around your index finger, pressing together the two opposite corners and pushing the third corner towards the outside at the same time (see figg. 1-3, p. 16).
Tortellini — A speciality from Emilia (Bologna), tortellini are traditionally served in broth, but are also excellent with a meat or tomato sauce.
To make tortellini, roll the filling into little balls and place them about 3-4 cm (1½ to 2 inches) apart and roughly 3-4 cm (1½ to 2 inches) from the edge of the dough. Lift the edge of the dough and fold it over the little mounds of filling. With a cutting-wheel, cut the dough close (not too close) to the filling to obtain a strip of stuffed pasta. Press down around the filling with your fingertips to seal. Run the cutting-wheel between the mounds of filling to cut the strip of pasta into small rectangles.

Lastly, draw one of the corners at the base of the rectangle over the other, shaping the pasta into a little hat (see figg. 4-8, pp. 17-18).

Ravioli — The most famous of all stuffed pastas. Once the term "raviolo" was used generally to describe any pasta wrapped around a filling. Ravioli are almost always square or rectangular in shape. To make them, place small mounds of filling (not too small because the best ravioli are those with the most filling) in a single row about 4 cm (2 inches) apart and 4 cm (2 inches) from the edge of the dough. Lift the outer edge of the dough and fold it over the mounds of filling. Using a pasta cutting-wheel, cut the dough close (but not too close) to the filling to make a strip of stuffed pasta. Press around the filling with your fingertips to seal the dough tightly. Finally, use the wheel again to cut the strip into farily large rectangles (see figg. 9-12, pp. 18-19).

Ravioli may be stuffed in several ways, then served with a sauce that complements the filling. "Ravioli alla genovese" are typically Ligurian and are made with paper-thin dough (using very few eggs and a lot of water) so that they cook in five minutes. They are round and stuffed with meat, vegetables or fish. Fish ravioli may be served in strained fish stock. Pansotti or "pot bellies" are another type of Ligurian ravioli. They are meatless ravioli in the shape of even-sided triangles filled with cheese, eggs and wild herbs, and served in a walnut sauce.

Another well-known variety of ravioli are the half-moon "cason-sei" from Brescia, named perhaps after the cheese with which they are dressed. They are fairly large, round or square envelopes of dough sometimes made like large tortellini.

Cappelletti — When finished they look like little hats ("cappellini"), but the method for making them is practically the same as that for making tortellini. They should be served in beef or chicken broth. In Romagna, where they originated, it is customary to serve them in capon broth for Christmas dinner.

Agnolotti — A speciality from Piedmont, agnolotti are generally square and stuffed with meat. They are usually served "dry" in a sauce based on the roasts or braised meat used in making the filling. There are numerous variations as families often make them on Mondays, using Sunday leftovers.

1
Cut the dough with a cutting-wheel into 4 cm (1¾ inch) squares.

2
Place a little filling in the middle of each square and fold the dough diagonally to form a triangle, press the edges firmly and...

3
... roll the filled triangle around your index finger, pinching the corners together.

4
Place small heaps of filling on the dough, about 3 to 4 cm (1¼ to 1¾ inches) apart.

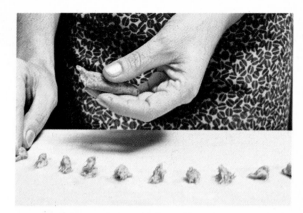

5
Fold the edge of the dough over the small heaps of filling.

6
Use the cutting-wheel to cut the stuffed dough into a long strip.

7
Press the pasta round each filling to seal well, then cut the filled dough strip into rectangles.

8
Overlap the two corners at the base of the rectangles, press them together and bend up the opposite corner.

9
Fold the edge of the dough over the heaps of filling placed at an even distance.

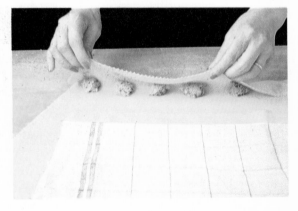

10
Trim along the edge of the folded dough, not too close to the filling, using the pasta cutting-wheel.

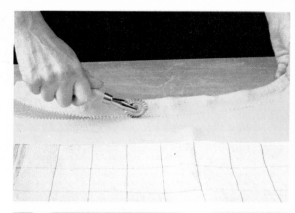

11
Using your fingertips, seal the dough around the filling.

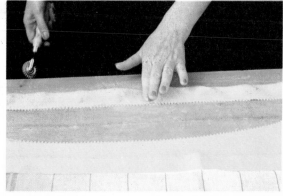

12
Cut the strip into fairly large rectangles, and your ravioli are ready.

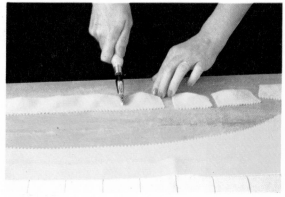

NECESSARY UTENSILS

Very few things are necessary for making pasta at home: a marble slab or wooden pastry-board, a rolling-pin... and two strong arms. Rolling out the dough very thin, as the skilful Emilian housewives still often do, needs a lot of strength and patience!

But time marches on and many housewives have replaced their rolling-pins with rolling-out machines, first manually then electrically driven. Blenders and even fully automatic machines with blenders incorporated to carry out the whole process from the flour to any shape of pasta one may desire are the latest models on the market (see figg. pp. 24-25).

The manual machine with a handle remains the most widely used of all, being reasonably priced and very easy to use. This machine has smooth rollers for rolling out and grooved rollers for making tagliatelle and tagliolini. The space between the two rollers is narrowed by turning the wheel on the side of the machine to obtain thinner dough at every click.

The electric machine works in the same way but with an electric motor. Usually the same motor drives several accessories. With the electric blenders it simply suffices to put the ingredients into the bowl provided, put on the lid and switch on. Small blades then turn slowly, mixing everything until a smooth and compact dough is formed, ready for whatever use is intended.

The most automatic machines are supplied with small discs for producing the various pasta shapes. The flour is poured into the special basin and the eggs dropped in one at a time while the machine is working. Once a compact dough has been made, a shutter comes down and the finished pasta comes out.

There are, in short, many types of pasta-making machines on the market today; each has its own particular features and needs precise quantities in order to perform well. Follow the instructions included with each machine very closely the first time; once you have gained experience you can make personal variations.

Special round or square pasta-cutting stamps may be used to cut stuffed dough into the required shape or, alternatively, the traditional serrated pasta-cutting wheel, or even an ordinary knife for straight edges.

20

The special metal trays with ravioli-shaped sections available in shops are an enormous boon for making ravioli. To use them, you simply unroll a sheet of dough over the ravioli tray, ease the dough into each ravioli dent, press it down gently round the edges with your fingertips to help it stick to the sides.

Now you can section with your chosen filling, which you will

1
Unroll a rectangular sheet of home-made dough over the special ravioli tray.

2
With floured fingers, press round the edges of each hollow to help the dough stick to the tray.

3
Place small heaps of filling on the dough into each hollow in the tray.

4
Cover with a second layer of dough the same size as the first.

5
Seal with the special, short rolling-pin, making sure that the two sheets of dough stick together.

have prepared beforehand, and cover with the second sheet of dough. Seal the ravioli by repeatedly passing the small rolling-pin (sold together with the tray) over the two sheets of dough.
In this way you will make one raviolo in each section of the tray (see figg. 1-5, on these pages).
There is a handy, ravioli-making accessory which fits onto the manual pasta-making machines. It has a container into which you put the filling, and a roller so designed that as the sheet of dough passes it is filled and directly acquires the raviolo shape.

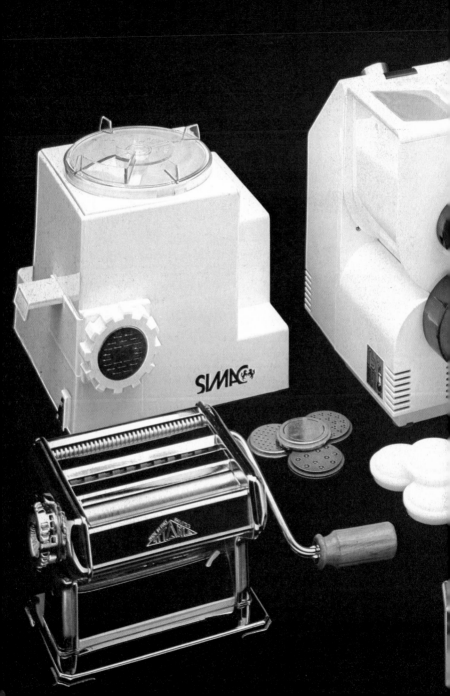

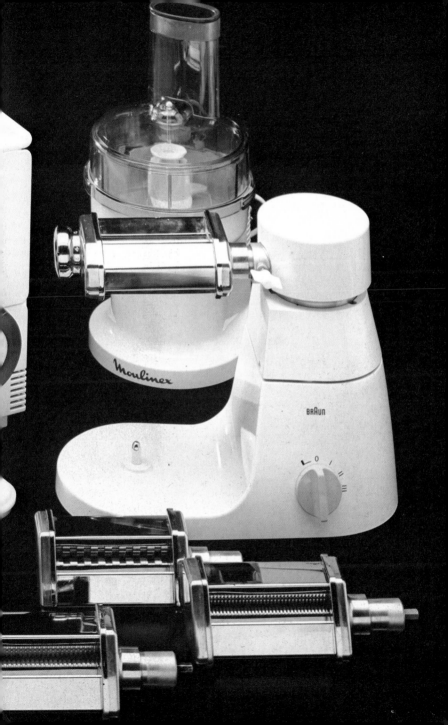

COLOURED PASTA

Green pasta — Quantities for 4 persons: 400 g (14 oz) plain, white flour, 200 g (7 oz) fresh spinach, 3 eggs , salt.
Cook the spinach for 5 to 10 minutes using only the water left on the leaves after washing, stirring all the time with a wooden spoon. Allow to cool, squeeze by hand and pass through a vegetable mill. Heap the flour on a pastry-board, make a "crater" in the centre, break in the eggs, add the spinach and a pinch of salt and mix. The amount of flour may be increased if the dough is too soft. Knead the ingredients together vigorously and proceed as for ordinary pasta. Green pasta can be used together with ordinary egg pasta to prepare dishes of "paglia e fieno" ("straw and hay") as well as exquisite baked pasta dishes.

Red pasta — Quantities for 4: 400 g (14 oz) white flour, 250 g (9 oz) carrots, 3 eggs, salt, one teaspoonful of tomato paste.
Scrape and dice the carrots, then boil until tender in a little salted water. Sieve them through a vegetable mill and dry the pureé in a small saucepan over low heat, stirring with a wooden spoon. Add the tomato paste. Proceed as for ordinary pasta, heaping the flour on the board and adding the eggs and mashed carrots.

Violet pasta — Quantities for 4: 400 g (14 oz) white flour, 1 medium-sized beetroot, 2 eggs and a pinch of salt. Buy ready-cooked beetroot, cut it up and pass it through a vegetable mill. Squeeze the beetroot well to extract as much juice as possible, then add the juice, eggs and salt to the flour. The amount of flour will vary according to the amount of juice obtained. Proceed as for other pastas. This pasta too cannot be rolled very thin and dries out very quickly. To avoid this, sprinkle it with yellow maize flour or semolina when you roll it out to cut it.

Orange pasta — Quantities for 4: 400 g (14 oz) white flour, 400 g (14 oz) pumpkin, 2 eggs and a pinch of salt. Slice the pumpkin and bake it for about an hour, or boil it in salted water for 30 minutes. Remove the peel and seeds and pass it through a vegetable mill. If the pulp is too liquid, dry it in a saucepan over a low heat, stirring rapidly with a wooden spoon. Knead the pumpkin together with the flour, eggs and salt as for other pastas.

INDUSTRIALLY MADE PASTA

Dry pasta is produced exclusively from durum wheat flour. When durum wheat is milled, an amber-coloured, rather granulous semolina is obtained, together with a finer version called "semolato".

The quality of industrially made pasta depends on the right choice of semolina blends used and the quantity and quality of protein-rich glutens the flour contains.

The gluten is the part of the flour which is insoluble in water and "binds" the starch both during production and whilst the pasta is being cooked, giving the "al dente" consistency desired (meaning it is not overcooked and therefore too soft).

Semolina is very difficult to mix with water (in fact it is almost impossible to knead it). This is why, in the most modern factories, after being sieved it is kneaded in automatic presses built for the purpose. To obtain constant results, the quantities of ingredients used in this process never vary. From here the dough is sent through a compression chamber, at the end of which a special die cuts it into the required form.

The last and perhaps most delicate process is drying. This too is done mechanically and in an air-conditioned environment. The dried pastas' water content must not exceed 12.5% or they will mould and turn acid.

The enormous pasta "family" existing on the market can be divided into three main groups:

long pastas: vermicelli, spaghetti, maccheroni, bucatini, zite, linguine, bavette, capellini;

short pastas: penne rigate or lisce (grooved or smooth quills), mezze penne (half quills), rigatoni (fluted tubes), farfalle (butterflies or bows), conchiglioni (large shells), pipe rigate (grooved tubes), mezze maniche (short sleeves), torciglioni (curly-whirlies), gnocchi, gramigna ecc;

tiny pastas: stelline (little stars), anellini (tiny rings), conchigliette (small shells), quadrettini (little squares), lancette, risoni, farfalline (tiny butterflies), pennette (small quills), etc.

Apart from the above-mentioned types of pasta, made simply

from water and semolina flour, an ever-increasing number of commercially produced pastas with eggs added are available to the consumer. There are two distinct kinds: "egg pasta", which must contain 5 eggs per kilo of semolina flour; and "pasta with eggs added", which must include at least 2 eggs per kilo of semolina.

Pasta with glutens or plasmon added for variation or special diets can also be found, together with pastas based on traditional home-made regional recipes: for example, "orecchiette" ("little ears") from Puglia; "gnocchetti" from Sardinia; and tagliatelle and lasagne from Emilia.

Ideal features of good industrial pasta — Before buying pasta it is advisable to check it carefully for the following features: it should be amber-coloured, slightly transparent, with an occasional dark trace of bran residue visible when held up to the light.

Long pasta should have a certain elasticity and short pasta should not snap too easily.

All types of pasta should appear almost translucent, neither floury nor opaque. The cooking water should remain fairly clear, turning only slightly cloudy and free of floury deposits. When cooked the pasta should keep its pale yellow hue, it must not become mushy, crack or turn gluey and it should triple in volume.

Should commercial pasta be adulterated by the addition of other less-refined cereals or even potato-flour, the evidence will be clear after cooking, as the pasta looses its elasticity and tastes floury.

Occasionally natural colourants (like curcuma or saffron) are used to tint egg pasta, or the eggs are replaced by the addition of egg powder of dubious origin.

Cooking rules — Making a good plate of pasta depends not only on the quality of the pasta used but also on following a few basic rules, for example:

— pasta needs to cook in plenty of water, roughly 1 litre (2 pints) for every 100 g ($3\frac{1}{2}$ oz);

— add the salt to the boiling water before putting in the pasta, using one teaspoonful per litre (2 pints) of water (cooking salt is best);

— a fairly low-sided, wide-based pan is best, to enable the heat to spread rapidly and help the water to come to the boil again quickly once the pasta has been added;

— add the pasta only when the water is boiling rapidly and mix it straight away with a ladle or wooden spoon; this stops it sticking together (especially spaghetti) or sticking to the bottom of the pan (like shorter, smaller pasta); adding a drop or two of oil to the water further prevents sticking;

— cook without a lid over high (but not excessive) heat;

— choose the most suitable type of pasta for each dish: short pasta is best with meat-sauces, pasta pies and baked pasta dishes; long pasta goes well with almost all kinds of sauce;

— cooking time depends on the type of pasta being used (from a minimum of 4-5 minutes to a maximum of 20-25); the only way to test is by tasting from time to time; drain when "al dente", i.e. done but still firm to the bite;

— drain as soon as the pasta is cooked and add the sauce in a warmed serving dish; some cooks advise adding 2 or 3 tablespoonfuls of cooking water before mixing in the sauce.

PASTA RECIPES

Agnolini in cream sauce *(serves 4)*

Pasta ingredients:
a sheet of pasta dough made
from 400 g (14 oz) white
flour and 4 eggs

Filling ingredients:
250 g (9 oz) turkey or chicken
50 g (2 oz) Parma ham
100 g (3½ oz) ricotta cheese
75 g (2½ oz) grated parmesan
cheese
1 slice Bologna sausage
2 chicken livers
2 tbsp. bread-crumbs

1 egg
2 sage leaves
2 tbsp. Marsala wine
1 tbsp. olive oil
nutmeg
pepper, salt

Sauce ingredients:
50 g (2 oz) butter
50 g (2 oz) grated parmesan
cheese
2 sage leaves
200 ml (6 fl oz) cooking cream
pepper, salt

Time needed: 2 hrs. 15 min.

First prepare the filling. Brown the sliced poultry, Parma ham
and Bologna sausage (Mortadella) in the butter and oil, season,
add the sage and chicken livers then douse with Marsala.
When the wine has evaporated remove the sage and mince the
meat. Add the ricotta, parmesan, bread-crumbs, egg and a
pinch of nutmeg. Mix and add salt if necessary. Use the dough
and the filling to prepare "agnolini" as described on p. 14.
Boil the agnolini in plenty of salted water and prepare the sauce
while they are cooking. To make the sauce, melt the butter with
the sage, add the cream, salt and pepper and heat thoroughly.
Drain the agnolini and tip them into a serving bowl; dress them
in layers with the hot cream and grated parmesan.
Leave them for two minutes to soak up the dressing, then serve.

Agnolini in vol-au-vent *(serves 6)*

Pasta and vol-au-vent
ingredients:
400 g (14 oz) home-made or
frozen puff pastry
a sheet of dough made from
400 g (14 oz) white flour
and 4 eggs

Filling ingredients:
250 g (9 oz) chicken breast
50 g (2 oz) Parma ham
150 g (5½ oz) mascarpone or
cream cheese
1 egg and 1 egg-yolk
2 tbsp. grated parmesan
cheese

30 g (1 oz) butter
a little brandy
freshly ground pepper, salt

Sauce ingredients:
70 g (2½ oz) butter
200 g (7 oz) boiled peas
(fresh, frozen or tinned)
80 g (3 oz) diced boiled ham
100 ml (3 fl oz) cooking
cream
½ tbsp. beef extract
½ small onion
3 tbsp. grated parmesan
cheese
freshly ground pepper, salt

Time needed: 2 hrs.

First make the vol-au-vent (if you use frozen pastry dough thaw it well before beginning). Roll the dough to a thickness of about ½ cm (¼ inch). Using the lid of a 25 cm (10 inch) pan as a guide, cut out a circle of dough using a sharp knife held at an angle. Wrap the pastry around the rolling-pin and place it on a lightly buttered baking-sheet, top-side-down. Centre another lid about 15 cm (6 inches) in diameter over the pastry circle and make a shallow incision with the knife all the way around, cutting about half-way into the dough. Now use the blunt edge of the knife to make shallow vertical dents around the outside edge of the dough. Brush the dough with beaten egg-yolk and cook in an oven pre-heated to 190°C/375°F/Gas 5 for about 25 minutes. Then lift the inner circle of the pastry shell out with a fork and place it upside-down on a plate (you will use it later as a lid). Scrape out part of the soft dough inside the pastry shell and place it in the oven for a further 5 minutes; take it out of the oven and leave it to cool.

Now make the filling for the agnolini. Sauté the minced Parma ham in 2 tablespoons of butter, add the chicken breast and brown over moderate heat, sprinkling from time to time with a little brandy. Mince the cooked chicken and place in a bowl together with its cooking juices, add the mascarpone (or cream cheese), an egg, the parmesan and a pinch of salt and freshly ground pepper. Mix the filling well and drop it in small mounds on the sheet of home-made dough. You should make agnolini about 2 to 3 cm (1 to 1½ inches) square as described on p. 14.

For the sauce, melt 70 g (2½ oz) butter in a large frying-pan and sauté the chopped onion gently; add the diced boiled ham, the peas and the beef extract dissolved in a little hot water. Mix well, cook for about 10 minutes, then add the cream.

Cook the agnolini in a generous amount of salted, boiling water, drain when still "al dente" and pour into the pan with the peas. Add the parmesan, a generous pinch of salt and freshly ground pepper, mix and tip the mixture into the pastry case (ready and waiting on its plate).

Place back in the oven for about 10 minutes, then serve the vol-au-vent with its lid on.

Agnolotti Piedmont style *(serves 4)*

Pasta ingredients:
a sheet of dough made from
    400 g (14 oz) white flour,
    4 eggs and 100 ml (3 fl oz)
    water

300 g (10 oz) spinach
1 egg
3 tbsp. grated parmesan cheese
nutmeg
pepper, salt

Filling ingredients:
250 g (9 oz) braised beef
100 g (3½ oz) roast pork
50 g (2 oz) Italian sausage
100 g (3½ oz) calves' brains
30 g (1 oz) butter

For cooking and dressing:
100 g (3½ oz) butter
grated parmesan cheese
juice or gravy from roast
    or braised meat
skimmed meat broth

Time needed: 2 hrs.

Boil, squeeze, chop and dry the spinach in a pan with the butter over moderate heat.

Lightly scald the calves' brains and the sausage, then mince with all the meat and place in a bowl. Add the spinach, grated cheese, pinches of salt and pepper and a sprinkle of nutmeg and bind the mixture with the egg. It should be thick but soft.

Divide the sheet of dough into two parts and place hazel-nut-sized balls of filling on one sheet, about 4 cm (2 inches) apart. Cover with the other sheet of dough and press down with two fingers between the mounds of filling. Cut out square agnolotti with a cutting-wheel or stamp. Boil them in a generous amount of broth, drain when slighlty "al dente" and dress with the butter, the juice or gravy of roast or braised meat and the grated cheese. Toss briefly in a frying-pan and serve.

Agnolotti with meat filling *(serves 4)*

Pasta ingredients:
a sheet of dough made from
   400 g (14 oz) white flour
   and 4 eggs

Filling ingredients:
300 g (10 oz) minced veal
30 g (1 oz) butter
50 g (2 oz) Parma ham
100 g (3½ oz) Bologna sausage
30 g (1 oz) grated parmesan
   cheese
1 egg
1 small onion
1 tbsp. beef extract
dry white wine
2 tbsp. olive oil
nutmeg, pepper, salt

Sauce ingredients:
200 g (7 oz) minced beef
400 g (14 oz) strained, mashed,
   tinned tomatoes
30 g (1 oz) bacon or bacon fat
20 g (¾ oz) dried boletus
   mushrooms
70 g (2½ oz) grated parmesan
   cheese
1 small onion
1 stick celery
1 clove garlic
1 bay leaf
1 clove
half a glass of dry
   white wine
olive oil
pepper, salt

Time needed: 3 hrs.

Make the sauce first. Finely chop the bacon, celery, onion and garlic and fry gently in a few tablespoons of olive oil. Add the minced beef, season with salt and pepper and brown over low heat. Add the bay leaf, clove and the mushrooms (previously soaked in warm water for 30 minutes, squeezed and chopped). Cook for a few minutes, douse with half a glass of dry white wine and allow to evaporate. Add the strained, sieved tomatoes and continue cooking over very low heat.

Now make the filling: finely chop the onion, Bologna sausage (Mortadella) and Parma ham; fry them gently in butter and two tablespoons of olive oil. When golden brown add the minced veal and the crumbled Italian sausage and brown well. After a few minutes pour in half a glass of white wine, let it evaporate, then salt and pepper and add the beef extract diluted in a little warm water. Cook until the mixture thickens. Remove from the heat, add the parmesan, allow to cool, then add the egg and a sprinkle of grated nutmeg, mixing thoroughly. Use the dough and the filling to make agnolotti as described on p. 15. Boil in salted water for 20 minutes before serving, taking care to add 1 tablespoon of olive oil to the cooking water; drain with care, place in a warm serving bowl or tureen and dress in layers with melted butter, the hot meat sauce and grated parmesan.

Bavette with fisherman's sauce *(serves 4)*

Pasta ingredients:
400 g (14 oz) bavette made
   from 400 g (14 oz) white
   flour and 4 eggs

Sauce ingredients:
450 g (1 lb) different varieties
   of fish (including gutted
   and cleaned shell-fish)
1 small bunch parsley

1 large onion
1 stick celery
1 clove garlic
1 bay leaf
juice of 1 lemon
1 carrot
1 tbsp. tomato paste
½ cup dry white wine
6 tbsp. olive oil
freshly ground pepper, salt

Time needed: 1 hr. 15 min.

Prepare a court-bouillon with ½ litre (1 pint) of cold water, ½ glass of dry white wine, the bay leaf, a sprig of parsley, ½ the onion (sliced), the stick of celery (cut lengthwise), the lemon juice and ½ teaspoon of salt. Bring to the boil and add the fish, already gutted and cleaned. When cooked, drain the fish from the stock and sieve to remove the bones, etc. Sieve the stock separately, pour into a saucepan, dilute with ½ litre (1 pint) water, boil and use to cook the bavette.

Meanwhile chop the remaining onion together with a few sprigs of parsley. Fry gently in the oil using an earthenware casserole until slightly golden, then add the tomato paste, thinned with half a ladle of the fish stock being used to cook the pasta. Reduce the sauce over moderate heat, stirring frequently. Add the sieved fish pieces, mixing thoroughly but gently. Sprinkle with freshly ground pepper.

Drain the pasta cooked "al dente", tip into a large serving dish containing the sauce, mix carefully and serve.

Bavette with fava bean sauce *(serves 4)*

Pasta ingredients:	60 g (2 oz) Parma ham
300 g (10 oz) bavette made from 300 g (10 oz) white flour and 3 eggs	60 g (2 oz) butter
	½ onion
	1 cup meat stock
	olive oil
Sauce ingredients:	freshly ground pepper
300 g (10 oz) shelled fava beans	salt

Time needed: 1 hr. 30 min.

Brown the chopped onion in 4 tablespoons of olive oil over moderate heat. Add the beans, moisten with a little stock and cook over moderate heat, adding more stock if necessary. Just before the beans are completely cooked, boil the pasta until cooked "al dente" and tip into a warmed serving bowl. When the beans are fully cooked, leave them over the heat and add the ham, cut into strips, stirring carefully. Season with salt and

Agnolotti with meat filling (p. 34)

freshly ground pepper and spread over the pasta together with small knobs of butter and freshly grated parmesan. Mix gently and serve straight away.

Bigoli with chicken giblets *(serves 4)*

Pasta ingredients:
bigoli made from
   350 g (12 oz)
   wholemeal flour
30 g (1 oz) butter
3 eggs
milk
salt

Sauce ingredients:
250 g (9 oz) chicken
   giblets (cut into small
   pieces)
7 tbsp. butter
½ tbsp. chopped sage
grated parmesan cheese
salt

Time needed: 2 hrs. 30 min.

Bigoli are a typical Venetian or Mantuan pasta. To make them, heap the flour on the pastry-board, make a hollow in the centre and break in the eggs. Add the melted butter and a pinch of salt. Knead, adding just the amount of milk you need to obtain a thickish dough. Pass the dough through a "bigoli-maker" (an old-fashioned, manual press) to make long, solid strings of pasta with a granulous texture, rather like large spaghetti. If you do not have a press, an ordinary manual pasta machine will do. Cut the bigoli into 30 cm (12 inch) lengths, using a floured knife, as they come out of the machine. Spread them out, wide apart, on the pastry-board and leave them to dry, but not too much. Now warm the butter with the sage leaves, add the giblets (except for the livers), salt and cook for about 20 minutes over moderate heat. Add a little chicken broth should the mixture become too dry. Just before removing from the heat add the livers and sauté until they stiffen.
Boil the bigoli in plenty of salted water, drain when "al dente" and toss with the sauce and cheese.

Bigoli with sardines *(serves 4)*

Pasta ingredients:
bigoli made with
   400 g (14 oz) wholemeal
   flour
2 tbsp. butter
4 eggs
milk
salt

Sauce ingredients:
300 g (10 oz) fresh sardines
   (if not available tinned
   will do)
1 clove garlic
3 tbsp. olive oil
freshly ground pepper
salt

Time needed: 1 hr. 30 min.

Prepare the bigoli as for "Bigoli with chicken giblets" (p. 38).
For the sauce: clean, bone, wash and dry the sardines. Crush the garlic clove and sauté in oil; remove the garlic when golden brown, mash the sardines and add to the oil. Cook slowly (do not fry) over moderate heat.
Cook the bigoli in a generous amount of salted boiling water, drain when "al dente", pour into a warmed serving bowl, add the hot sardine sauce, a sprinkle of freshly ground pepper, stir briskly and serve piping hot.

Bigoli with anchovy sauce *(serves 4)*

400 g (14 oz) home-made
   bigoli

Sauce ingredients:
50 g (2 oz) tinned anchovies

250 g (9 oz) sweet onions
   (yellow type)
4 tbsp. olive oil
black pepper
salt

Time needed: 1 hr. 30 min.

Prepare the bigoli as for "Bigoli with chicken giblets" (p. 38).
Slice the onions thinly and fry gently in 3 tablespoons of olive oil using an earthenware dish. As they begin to brown, add a little

water, cover the dish and cook slowly until they become shapeless and soft.

Now add the tinned anchovies (drained), and mash them into a pulp with a fork.

Cook for another two minutes, add a tablespoon of cold olive oil, stir and turn off the heat.

Cook the bigoli in salted boiling water, drain when "al dente", pour into a serving dish, add the sauce, a pinch of freshly ground black pepper and serve.

Bucatini with amatriciana sauce *(serves 4)*

400 g (14 oz) bucatini

Sauce ingredients:
100 g (3½ oz) salted pork or bacon (diced)
1 small piece onion

100 g (3½ oz) strained, tinned tomatoes
1 small piece hot red pepper
olive oil
salt

Time needed: 30 min.

Heat 4 tablespoons of olive oil in a pan, add the diced salted pork (or bacon) and stir them in the oil thoroughly until golden brown.

Remove and drain off excess oil; put on a plate and keep warm.

Add the finely chopped onion and the piece of red pepper to the hot fat left in the pan.

When the onion begins to brown, add the strained tomato pulp cut into pieces, salt and leave to cook for 5 minutes stirring all the time.

While finishing to cook the sauce, boil the bucatini in a generous amount of salted water, drain when "al dente" and pour into the pan with the sauce.

Add the cubes of browned salted pork (or bacon) and cook the pasta in the sauce for another 2 minutes. Remove from the heat and serve immediately.

Bucatini with mussel sauce *(serves 4)*

400 g (14 oz) bucatini

Sauce ingredients:
800 g (1¾ lb) mussels
50 g (2 oz) green and black
  olives
50 g (2 oz) butter

1 clove garlic
250 g (9 oz) whole,
  skinned tomatoes (tinned)
1 tbsp. chopped parsley
2-3 anchovy fillets
  (or 1 tbsp. anchovy paste)
olive oil, salt

Time needed: 1 hr. 30 min.

Scrub and clean the mussels, washing them carefully under running water, then heat them in a frying-pan with one tablespoon of olive oil until they open. Remove each mussel from its shell and place them in a separate dish. Carefully filter the water left in the pan after cooking and add to the mussels.

Using an earthenware casserole, warm half the butter, 2 to 3 tablespoons of olive oil, then add the anchovy fillets cut into pieces (or the anchovy paste); heat until the anchovies disintegrate (in the case of the fillets), then add the olives (stoned), the skinned tomatoes and the cooking water left from the mussels. Heat gently to thicken the sauce, then add the mussels, the finely chopped garlic and the chopped parsley.

While finishing the sauce, boil the bucatini in a generous amount of salted water, add a drop of cold water to halt the cooking process, drain and dress in a serving bowl with a large knob of butter and half the sauce. Pour the remaining sauce into a sauce-boat to be used at table and serve the pasta at once.

This sauce is equally appetizing served with spaghetti.

Bucatini with olives *(serves 4)*

400 g (14 oz) bucatini

Sauce ingredients:
1 small onion

100 g (3½ oz) green olives
  (preferably Spanish)
1 tbsp. finely chopped
  parsley

1 finely chopped clove
   garlic
350 g (12 oz) tinned,
   skinned tomatoes
½ yellow or green pepper

5 tbsp. olive oil
2 tbsp. grated parmesan
   cheese
freshly ground black
   pepper, salt

Time needed: 1 hr.

Scorch the pepper over a flame (or roast in the oven); peel off
the burnt skin and remove the seeds and stringy insides. Drain
and seed the tomatoes. Gently fry the finely chopped onion and
garlic in the olive oil and add the coarsely chopped pepper.
Brown for 10 minutes, then add the tomatoes, mashed with a
fork. Stir and thicken over low heat for about 30 minutes.
Season with salt and freshly ground pepper and mix in 50 g (2
oz) of stoned, halved olives. Stir and leave over the heat a
further 10 minutes. Add the chopped parsley at the last minute,
mixing carefully.
When the sauce is almost ready, cook the bucatini in a generous
amount of salted, boiling water, drain when "al dente" and dress
with the sauce. Pour into a serving dish, garnish with the deep
remaining olives and the grated parmesan cheese and serve
immediately.

Bucatini in tomato cream sauce *(serves 4)*

400 g (14 oz) bucatini

Sauce ingredients:
150 g (5½ oz) skinned
   tomatoes (fresh
   or tinned)
50 g (2 oz) butter
30 g (1 oz) flour
3 tbsp. grated

parmesan cheese
250 ml (8 fl oz) milk
½ glass cooking
   cream
1 generous pinch dried
   marjoram
nutmeg
salt
pepper

Time needed: 40 min.

Begin by heating the milk and sieving the tomatoes. Then melt 40 g (1½ oz) butter in a pan, add the flour, stirring gently with a wooden spoon, pour in the hot milk a little at a time and mix with the flour and butter, stirring continuously over moderate heat until the sauce turns smooth. Add the cream and the sieved tomatoes. After mixing carefully to blend the ingredients, add the salt, pepper and nutmeg; remove from the heat and keep warm in a basin over a saucepan of hot water (bain-marie).

Boil the bucatini in a generous amount of salted water, drain when "al dente" and dress with the sauce, the rest of the butter and the grated parmesan. Stir, rub the dried marjoram between your fingers and sprinkle over the pasta, then serve straight away.

Cannelloni with mascarpone *(serves 4)*

Pasta ingredients:
a sheet of dough prepared
   from 400 g (14 oz)
   white flour and 4 eggs

Filling ingredients:
200 g (7 oz) ricotta cheese
200 g (7 oz) mascarpone (or
   cream cheese)
70 g (2½ oz) grated

fontina cheese
300 g (10 oz) spinach or beet
   leaves
50 g (2 oz) butter
25 g (1 oz) white flour
12 thin slices fontina cheese
250 ml (8 fl oz) cooking
   cream
freshly ground pepper
salt

Time needed: about 2 hrs.

Boil, squeeze dry and mill the spinach; place it in a bowl, add the ricotta, mascarpone (or cream cheese), freshly ground pepper and salt. Mix carefully. Melt 30 g (1 oz) butter in a pan, add the flour, salt and, very gradually, the cream. Stir without bringing to the boil. Remove from the heat and add half the grated fontina.

Cut the sheet of pasta into 12 cm (5 inch)-sided squares. Boil these in salted water, drain and spread on a clean tea-towel to

Bucatini with mussel sauce (p. 42)

dry. Cover each with a slice of fontina, place a little filling in the centre and spread it evenly with a spatula.

Roll up each square into a cannellone and arrange them, seam-side-down, in a buttered, ovenproof dish. Coat with the remaining filling, the rest of the grated fontina and knobs of butter. Brown in a hot oven (190°C/375°F/Gas 5) and serve.

Cannelloni with giblets *(serves 4)*

Pasta ingredients:
a sheet of dough made from
   400 g (14 oz) white flour
   and 4 eggs

Filling ingredients:
150 g (5½ oz) chicken gizzards
150 g (5½ oz) chicken livers
100 g (3½ oz) mascarpone (or
   cream cheese)
100 g (3½ oz) ricotta cheese

40 g (1½ oz) white flour
80 g (3 oz) grated parmesan
   cheese
2 egg-yolks
1 small onion
1 handful parsley
500 ml (1 pt) milk
½ glass dry white wine
1 lemon
pepper
salt

Time needed: 2 hrs. 15 min.

Soak the gizzards for about 30 minutes in cold water; skin them, then scald them in boiling water containing a knob of butter and a squeeze of lemon juice. Gently brown the chopped onion in 30 g (1 oz) butter; clean and chop the chicken livers (checking for, and removing, any gall bladders); chop the gizzards and add them, together with the livers, to the onion. Season with salt and pepper and douse with the wine; cook thoroughly, sprinkling with chopped parsley just before removing from the heat.

Separately, sieve the ricotta into a bowl (or mash with a fork), add the mascarpone, half the grated parmesan and the giblets; check for salt and add if necessary.

Cut the sheet of dough into 12 cm (5 inch)-sided squares. Boil in plenty of salted water, drain when half-cooked and lay out on a clean tea-towel to dry. Place a blob of filling in the centre of each, spread out evenly with a spatula and roll up into cannelloni.

Put the milk on to boil. Melt 40 g (1½ oz) butter in a small pan, sieve and stir in the flour. Dilute gradually with the boiling milk, stirring all the time. Season with salt and pepper and simmer for a few minutes, stirring continuously. Now remove from the heat and add the remaining grated parmesan cheese and the 2 beaten egg-yolks, one at a time. Arrange the cannelloni, seam-side-down, in a buttered, ovenproof dish, cover with the béchamel and brown in a hot oven (190°C/375°F/Gas 5) for about 20 minutes. Serve piping hot.

Cannelloni with meat filling *(serves 4)*

Pasta ingredients:
a sheet of dough made from
   400 g (14 oz) white flour
   and 4 eggs

Filling ingredients:
100 g (3½ oz) roast veal
100 g (3½ oz) roast pork
100 g (3½ oz) cooked
   tongue
110 g (3¾ oz) butter

600 g (1¼ lb) spinach
180 g (6½ oz) grated parmesan
   cheese
50 g (2 oz) white flour
yolks of 2 hard-boiled eggs
2-3 tbsp. home-made tomato
   sauce or diluted tomato
   purée
500 ml (1 pt) milk
salt
pepper

Time needed: 2 hrs. 30 min.

Clean, wash, squeeze dry and chop the spinach. Melt 30 g (1 oz) butter in a pan and stir in the chopped spinach. Mince the roast meats and the tongue and mix in a basin together with the spinach, the tomato purée, 80 g (3 oz) grated parmesan and the 2 hard-boiled egg-yolks (mashed with a fork). Taste for salt and add any if necessary.
Boil the milk. Melt 50 g (2 oz) butter in a small pan, sieve and stir in the flour. Gradually dilute the mixture with the boiling milk, adding a little at a time and stirring continuously. Thicken, remove from the heat and season with salt and pepper. Stir in 2 tablespoons of tomato purée to the filling.

Cut the sheet of dough into 12 cm (5 inch)-sided squares. Boil in plenty of salted water, drain and lay on a clean tea-towel to dry. Drop a blob of filling in the centre of each, spread it out evenly with a spatula and roll up into cannelloni. Arrange the cannelloni in a buttered, ovenproof dish, cover with the sauce, the remaining grated parmesan and knobs of butter, and brown in a hot oven (190°C/375°F/Gas 5). Cannelloni are at their best taken from the oven and served straight away.

Cannolicchi with hard-boiled eggs *(serves 4)*

400 g (14 oz) cannolicchi	(or diluted tomato purée)
2 eggs	100 g (3½ oz) grated parmesan cheese
Sauce ingredients:	30 g (1 oz) butter
4 tbsp. tomato sauce	freshly ground pepper, salt

Time needed: 30 min.

Hard-boil the eggs; shell and slice them. Warm the home-made tomato sauce (or diluted purée). Boil the cannolicchi in salted water, drain when "al dente", pour into a serving dish and dress with the butter and hot tomato sauce. Sprinkle with the parmesan, the pepper and garnish with the slices of hard-boiled eggs. Serve straight away.

Cappellacci with chestnut filling *(serves 4)*

Pasta ingredients:	50 g (2 oz) grated parmesan cheese
a sheet of dough made from 400 g (14 oz) white flour and 4 eggs	1 egg
	olive oil, pepper, salt
Filling ingredients:	Sauce ingredients:
250 g (9 oz) dried chestnuts	300 g (10 oz) Italian sausage
300 g (10 oz) Italian sausage	25 g (1 oz) butter

70 g (2½ oz) grated parmesan cheese	tomatoes
	olive oil
250 g (9 oz) tinned skinned	pepper, salt

Time needed: 2 hrs. 30 min. (plus the time needed to soak the chestnuts).

Soak the chestnuts overnight. The day of preparation, boil in slightly salted water, drain and mash while hot.

Skin the sausage, brown gently in a little oil and break up with a fork. Add to the mashed chestnuts together with the grated parmesan, the egg, salt and pepper. Should the mixture seem too sloppy, some bread-crumbs will help it to dry and thicken.

Using a serrated cutter, stamp out 6 cm (2½ inch)-diameter discs from the sheet of pasta dough. Place a blob of filling in the middle of half the discs, and use the rest as covers, pressing round the edges of each to seal well. Twisting it round your index finger, bring together the opposite sides of the cappellaccio, overlap them and pinch them together.

Now for the sauce: cut the sausage into small pieces; fry gently in butter and 2 to 3 tablespoons of olive oil. Strain and sieve the tinned tomatoes, add together with salt and pepper and cook over low heat, stirring frequently. Boil the cappellacci for 15 minutes in a generous quantity of salted water, drain and pour into a serving dish. Add the sauce, the grated parmesan and serve hot.

Cappelletti Romagna style *(serves 4)*

Pasta ingredients:
a sheet of dough made from
    400 g (14 oz) white flour
    and 4 eggs

Filling ingredients:
200 g (7 oz) ricotta cheese
2 eggs

50 g (2 oz) grated parmesan
    cheese
nutmeg, salt

Dressing ingredients:
100 g (3½ oz) butter
100 g (3½ oz) grated
    parmesan cheese

Time needed: 2 hrs.

To make the filling, force the ricotta cheese through a sieve into a bowl. Add the parmesan, a whole egg plus the yolk of a second, a pinch of nutmeg, the salt, and stir well until smooth and creamy. Using the pasta dough and the cheese filling make the cappelletti following the instructions on p. 15. Boil them in plenty of salted water, drain and pour into a serving bowl.

Melt the butter in a pan and heat until hazel brown in colour; pour over the cappelletti, sprinkle with the grated parmesan, mix and serve.

Cappelletti in walnut sauce *(serves 4)*

Pasta ingredients:
a sheet of dough made from
    400 g (14 oz) white flour
    and 4 eggs

Filling ingredients:
500 g (1 lb) beet leaves
200 g (7 oz) minced beef
80 g (3 oz) butter
1 egg
1 slice bread (without crust)

a little milk

Sauce ingredients:
4 tbsp. grated parmesan
    cheese
1 cup shelled walnuts
2 tbsp. pine kernels
4 cloves garlic
2 tbsp. finely chopped basil
fresh marjoram
olive oil, salt, pepper

Time needed: 2 hrs.

Soak the slice of bread in a little milk. Boil the beet leaves in a little salted water, drain, squeeze dry and chop. Gently fry the minced beef in a pan with 30 g (1 oz) butter, add a sprinkle of chopped marjoram, the beet leaves and cook for about 10 minutes. Remove from the heat, add the egg, 2 tablespoons of grated parmesan, salt (if necessary), a pinch of pepper and the slice of bread (taken out of the milk and squeezed dry). Mix well. Use the pasta dough and the filling to prepare cappelletti as described on p. 15. Boil them in salted water, drain, tip into a serving bowl and keep warm. Chop the walnuts finely then pound them together with the pine kernels using a pestle and

mortar. Add the cloves of garlic and crush into a mushy pulp.
Melt the remaining butter in a pan, add a little oil and pour in the walnut mixture. Season with salt and pepper and remove from the heat. Now add the finely chopped basil and the left-over grated parmesan. Pour over the cappelletti, stir and serve immediately.

Casonsei Brescian style *(serves 4)*

Pasta ingredients:
a sheet of dough made from
   400 g (14 oz) white flour
   and 4 eggs

Filling ingredients:
300 g (10 oz) Italian sausage
100 g (3½ oz) grated
   parmesan cheese
1 bread roll (or 2 slices

of bread) without crust
a little milk
salt

Dressing ingredients:
100 g (3½ oz) butter
100 g (3½ oz) grated
   parmesan cheese
a few sage leaves
salt

Time needed: 1 hr. 30 min.

Break the bread (without crust) into pieces and soak in a little milk, squeeze and put into a bowl. Add the sausage cut into small pieces, the grated parmesan, salt to taste and stir well.
Cut the pasta dough into 8 × 12 cm (3 × 5 inch) rectangles. Place a blob of filling on each and fold lengthwise. Press firmly all round the edge of the filling. Take the ends of each rectangle and pull them downwards, giving each "raviolo" the shape of a pair of shorts (which is the meaning of "casonsei" in Brescian dialect).
Boil in an adequate amount of salted water, drain, pour into a serving bowl and dress with the hot butter, melted together with the sage leaves in a small pan. Sprinkle with the parmesan and serve.

Cavatieddi from Puglia *(serves 4)*

Pasta ingredients:
150 g (5½ oz) durum wheat

semolina, 200 g (7 oz)
white flour and salt

Sauce ingredients:
meat sauce, or tomato
sauce (or any other sauce
you prefer)

Time needed: 2 hrs. 30 min.

This is a traditional home-made dish from Puglia. Heap the two flours on the pastry-board, make a "crater" in the centre and blend together with tepid salted water, kneading until the dough strongly resembles that used for bread-making (slightly thicker perhaps, but no softer). Roll it out into 1 cm ($\frac{3}{8}$ inch)-thick, stringy "sausages" (about as thick as your little finger) and roughly 40 cm (16 inches) long.

It is wise to make no more than two "sausages" at a time and to keep the dough covered with a cloth while you are working as it tends to dry out quickly.

Chop each thin "sausage" into short pieces, pressing and pulling each with the floured point of a blunt knife to make the cavatieddi (or "tiny shells").

Leave them on the pastry-board to dry in the air.

Cook in plenty of salted boiling water, drain and serve with a tasty meat sauce, fresh tomatoes, basil and oil or simply (and typically Puglian) with chopped garlic, olive oil and chilli pepper.

Cialzons from Friuli *(serves 4)*

Pasta ingredients:
dough made from
   400 g (14 oz) durum
   wheat semolina
   and 4 eggs

Filling ingredients:
500 g (1 lb) floury potatoes
70 g (2½ oz) butter
25 g (1 oz) sugar
1 small onion
1 handful chopped parsley

a few mint leaves
½ wine glass brandy
powdered cinnamon
broth
nutmeg
salt
pepper

Dressing ingredients:
100 g (3½ oz) butter
100 g (3½ oz) grated
   parmesan cheese

Time needed: 2 hrs.

Blend the flour and eggs and knead for 15 minutes. Roll into a ball, cover with a cloth and leave to rest.

Boil the potatoes in slightly salted water, peel and mash in a bowl.

Add the chopped mint and parsley, sugar, brandy, salt and pepper. Mix in pinches of nutmeg and cinnamon.

Slice the onion, fry gently in the butter and remove, adding only the flavoured butter to the other ingredients. Stir well.

Roll out a thin sheet of pasta and cut out 5 cm (2 inch)-diameter circles. Place a blob of filling in the centre of each and fold over into a semi-circle. Boil the cialzons in broth, drain and serve piping hot with slightly browned melted butter and a generous sprinkling of grated parmesan. Stir gently and serve.

Ciriole from Umbria *(serves 4)*

Pasta ingredients:	Sauce ingredients:
a sheet of dough	400 g (14 oz) tomato pulp
made from 400 g (14 oz)	2 cloves garlic
durum wheat	1 chilli pepper
flour	3 tbsp. olive oil, salt

Time needed: 1 hr. 30 min.

To make this typically Umbrian dish, mix the flour with a pinch of salt and, adding only water, knead together until you obtain a rather firm dough. Work it hard for at least 15 minutes, slapping it down repeatedly onto the pastry-board. Roll it out into a rather thick sheet and cut it into 2 to 3 cm (1 to 1½ inch)-wide ribbons. With floured hands, carefully wind the pieces of pasta round thick knitting needles, leave them to dry a little, slip off and boil them.

Gently fry the chopped garlic and crushed hot pepper in hot olive oil. Add the mashed tomato pulp and a pinch of salt, then thicken the sauce over moderate heat. Drain the pasta and toss with the hot sauce before serving.

Conchiglie in cauliflower sauce *(serves 4)*

200 g (7 oz) conchiglie

Sauce ingredients:
1 fresh cauliflower
  (weighing) 1 kg (2 lb)
one 100 g (3½ oz) slice smoked

streaky bacon
250 g (9 oz) tomato pulp
100 g (3½ oz) grated
  parmesan cheese
2-3 cloves garlic
olive oil, salt

Time needed: 45 min.

Cut the cauliflower into pieces (not too small) and wash. Begin cooking the pasta in salted boiling water, adding the cauliflower pieces after 5 minutes. Cook them together.
Dice the bacon and brown in 4 or 5 tablespoons of olive oil. Add a pinch of salt and the chopped garlic; cook until golden brown and add the mashed tomato pulp. Cook for a further 5 minutes. Drain the pasta and the cauliflower both "al dente" and pour into an large serving bowl. Dress with the sauce and sprinkle with the grated parmesan. Leave to stand for two minutes and serve.

Conchiglie in frankfurter sauce *(serves 4)*

400 g (14 oz) conchiglie

Sauce ingredients:
4 frankfurter sausages
one 100 g (3½ oz) slice smoked
  streaky bacon

1 small onion
1 chilli pepper
250 g (9 oz) tinned skinned
  tomatoes
a few basil leaves
olive oil, salt

Time needed: 1 hr.

Lightly scald the frankfurters in boiling water, drain and cut them into rounds.
Chop the onion finely and cook gently until soft (but not brown) in 2-3 tablespoons of olive oil. Dice and add the bacon; brown

Conchiglie in frankfurter sauce and
Corzetti Ligurian style (p. 59)

and add the sliced frankfurters and the whole chilli pepper. Stir, leave for two minutes then add the mashed tomatoes, 4 or 5 basil leaves, salt to taste, cover and thicken over moderate heat, stirring occasionally.

Cook the pasta in plenty of salted boiling water, drain when "al dente", dress with the hot sauce and serve at once.

This sauce is just as tasty with rigatoni.

Conchiglioni with meatball sauce *(serves 4)*

400 g (14 oz) conchiglioni
   rigati

Sauce ingredients:
200 g (7 oz) minced beef
50 g (2 oz) butter
1 dry bread roll (without
   crust)
1 hard-boiled egg
1 raw egg

1 glass cooking cream
a few tablespoons milk
1 small bunch parsley
1 tbsp. chopped pickled
   pepper
2 tbsp. grated parmesan
   cheese
1 sprig sage
1 tbsp. olive oil
salt

Time needed: 1 hr. 30 min.

Soak the soft part of the bread roll in a little warm milk, squeeze it, and mash it in a bowl. Add the minced beef, the parmesan, the chopped parsley, the olive oil, the hard-boiled egg (cut up), the chopped pepper and a pinch of salt. Beat in the raw egg to bind the mixture and blend the ingredients well. Roll the mixture into meatballs the size of large olives.

Melt the butter in a pan and add the sage leaves. Fry gently then add the meatballs, turning and gently browning each. Lastly add the cream and 2 tablespoons of milk. Simmer over moderate heat until the meatballs are thoroughly done.

Cook the conchiglioni in a sufficient amount of boiling salted water, drain when "al dente", heat in the pan together with the meatball sauce, mixing carefully before serving.

Corzetti Ligurian style *(serves 4)*

Pasta ingredients:
300 g (10 oz) white flour,
  1-2 eggs and salt

Sauce ingredients:
75 g (2½ oz) butter

1 small handful pine kernels
1 pinch fresh marjoram
75 g (2½ oz) grated parmesan
  cheese
pepper
salt

Time needed: 1 hr.

Heap the flour on the pastry-board, make a "crater" in the middle, break in the eggs, add 2 to 3 pinches of salt and beat with a fork; gradually add a few tablespoons of warm water, enough to obtain a thick, firm dough. Knead well. Break off chick-pea-sized pieces of pasta, pull each out lengthwise and press on each end with two fingertips. The corzetti should look like filled-in figure eights. Spread them out on a clean cloth, not touching one another, and leave them to dry.
Boil a generous amount of salted water and cook the corzetti. Melt the butter in a pan and add the finely chopped marjoram. Drain the pasta with a perforated spoon or skimmer, place into a serving bowl and dress layer by layer with the heated butter, whole pine kernels, grated parmesan and a good sprinkle of freshly ground pepper. Stir and serve straight away. Corzetti are also delicious dressed with a meat or mushroom sauce.

Ditali rigati with haricot bean sauce *(serves 4)*

400 g (14 oz) ditali rigati

Sauce ingredients:
500 g (1 lb) fresh haricot beans
one 70 g (2½ oz) slice streaky
  smoked bacon
500 g (1 lb) ripe tomatoes or
  250 g (9 oz) tinned tomatoes

1 carrot
1 onion
1 stick celery
1 tbsp. chopped parsley
1 clove garlic
1 beef stock cube
40 g (1½ oz) butter
100 g (3½ oz) grated parmesan

Time needed: 3 hrs.

Finely chop the bacon, the carrot, the celery, the garlic and the onion.
Heat in an earthenware casserole with a few tablespoons of olive oil. Cook gently until the vegetables become soft and wilt, then add the beans and the tomatoes (peeled, their seeds removed and mashed with a fork). (If using tinned tomatoes remember to strain them first.) Cook for a few minutes then add the beef cube, dissolved in a cup of boiling water. Season with salt, pepper, cover and cook over low heat, stirring from time to time. Should the water evaporate excessively add more boiling water or stock as required.
Cook the pasta in a generous amount of boiling salted water; drain when "al dente", pour into a wide serving dish with knobs of butter. Before removing the sauce from the heat stir in the parsley. Pour over the pasta, mixing well. Serve hot with a generous sprinkle of grated parmesan.

Farfalle with salmon sauce *(serves 4)*

400 g (14 oz) home-made egg farfalle	salmon
	200 ml (6 fl oz) cooking cream
Sauce ingredients:	**1 tin red caviar**
150 g (5½ oz) smoked	salt

Time needed: 45 min.

Dice two or three slices of salmon and pulp the remainder. Cook the farfalle in a generous amount of salted boiling water, drain when "al dente", and heat the cream.
Use the hot cream to dilute the salmon pulp in a serving bowl. Add the pasta and carefully stir in the salmon pieces and the red caviar.
Serve immediately.

Farfalle with chicken livers *(serves 4)*

400 g (14 oz) home-made
  egg farfalle

Sauce ingredients:
250 g (9 oz) chicken livers
one thick slice smoked streaky
  bacon
400 g (14 oz) strained tinned
  tomatoes

50 g (2 oz) butter
70 g (2½ oz) grated parmesan
  cheese
1 small onion (chopped)
1 stick celery (chopped)
1 carrot (chopped)
½ cup dry white wine
olive oil
salt, pepper

Time needed: 1 hr. 30 min.

Halve the livers. Heat 2 tablespoons butter and 3 tablespoons of oil in a pan. Add the onion, celery and carrot; fry until they wilt. Dice the bacon and add together with the livers. Sauté slowly for 5 minutes. Pour in the wine and evaporate over moderate heat. Add the tomato pulp, salt and pepper and cook for a further 30 minutes. Boil the pasta, drain when "al dente", and toss in a serving bowl with the remaining butter. Stir in the sauce, sprinkle with the parmesan cheese and serve hot.

Fettuccine baked in the oven *(serves 4)*

400 g (14 oz) home-made egg
  fettuccine

Dressing ingredients:
1 small mozzarella cheese
100 g (3½ oz) butter

100 g (3½ oz) boiled ham
100 g (3½ oz) grated
  parmesan cheese
2-3 tbsp. bread crumbs
freshly ground pepper
salt

Time needed: 40 min.

Cook the fettuccine in a generous amount of boiling salted water, drain when "al dente" (keeping 2 tablespoons of the cooking water), dress with half the butter and parmesan, the 2 tablespoons of cooking water and a pinch of freshly ground pepper. Grease an ovenproof dish, sprinkle with the bread-crumbs and tip in half the fettuccine. Cover with a layer of thinly sliced mozzarella and thin strips of boiled ham and top with the rest of the fettuccine. Spread with knobs of butter and the remainder of the grated parmesan. Sprinkle with a few bread-crumbs and brown in a hot oven (200°C/400°F/Gas 6). Serve piping hot.

Fettuccine with Swiss cheese sauce *(serves 4)*

400 g (14 oz) home-made egg
   fettuccine

Sauce ingredients:
120 (4½ oz) grated Swiss
   gruyère cheese

80 g (3 oz) grated Swiss
   sbrinz cheese
50 g (2 oz) butter
100 ml (3 fl oz) whipped
   cream
freshly ground pepper, salt

Time needed: 30 min.

Cook the fettuccine in a generous amount of salted boiling water and in the meantime, make the cheese sauce. Heat the whipped cream in a pan over low heat; add the grated gruyère, stir gently until it melts, then add knobs of butter. Drain the fettuccine "al dente" and tip into a previously heated serving bowl. When the butter has liquified stir and pour the sauce over the pasta, sprinkle with the sbrinz and the ground pepper, stir and serve.

Fusilli Neaples style *(serves 4)*

400 g (14 oz) home-made
fusilli

Sauce ingredients:
400 g (14 oz) fresh (or
   strained tinned) tomatoes
150 g (5½ oz) mozzarella cheese

6 tbsp. olive oil
3 tbsp. grated pecorino
   cheese
1 pinch fresh oregano
   (dried if fresh not
   available)
freshly ground pepper, salt

Time needed: 35-40 min.

Wash and dry the fresh tomatoes; cut them into segments and remove the seeds (if using the tinned variety, strain, cut and remove the seeds).

Heat the oil in an earthenware casserole, add the tomato pieces, diced mozzarella, grated pecorino cheese and oregano. Season with a pinch of salt and freshly ground pepper, cover and cook over moderate heat for 10 minutes.

Now cook the fusilli in a generous amount of boiling salted water, drain when "al dente" and dress with the sauce in an ovenproof dish. Stir gently and bake in a hot oven (200°C/ 400°F /Gas 6) for 7 minutes before serving.

This sauce is equally delicious with spaghetti, bucatini, linguine and torciglioni.

Fusilli Syracuse style *(serves 4)*

400 g (14 oz) home-made fusilli	**3 cloves garlic (peeled and left whole)**
	1 large aubergine
Sauce ingredients:	**1 green pepper**
1 kg (2 lb) whole, fresh (or tinned) plum tomatoes	**1 tbsp. capers**
	1 small bunch parsley
30 g (1 oz) pitted black olives	**100 ml (3 fl oz) olive oil**
	freshly ground pepper
4 anchovy fillets	**salt**

Time needed: 1 hr.

Scorch the green pepper over a flame (or bake it in the oven, turning frequently), skin it and cut it into pieces, extracting the seeds and stringy insides. Dice the aubergine, peel and sieve the fresh tomatoes (or strain and sieve the tinned variety), and chop the parsley. Heat the oil in an earthenware casserole, add the cloves of garlic and remove when golden brown. Add the aubergine and the tomato pulp. Boil for 10 minutes, stirring

Fettuccine with Swiss cheese sauce (p. 63)

with a wooden spoon. Now add the pieces of green pepper, the capers, the olives, the anchovies (sliced into pieces), the chopped parsley, salt and pepper and cook gently for a further 7 minutes. Meanwhile boil the fusilli in plenty of salted water, drain when "al dente", dress with the hot sauce, stir and serve.

Fusilli with fresh vegetables *(serves 4)*

400 g (14 oz) home-made
  fusilli

Dressing ingredients:
200 g (7 oz) boiled peas
1 large ripe tomato

1 sweet fleshy pepper
  (red or yellow)
1 small bunch basil
1 tbsp. Worcestershire sauce
2 lemons
olive oil, salt

Time needed: 30 min. (plus 1 hr. standing in a cool place).

Cook the fusilli in a generous amount of salted boiling water. While the pasta is cooking, roast the pepper over a flame (or in the oven, turning frequently) and stroke off the scorched skin using a tea-towel. Remove the seeds and stringy insides, then dice and place in a rather large bowl. Add the diced tomato, the peas and the chopped basil. Drain the pasta when "al dente" and tip into the bowl. Add 6 tablespoons of oil, the juice of 2 lemons and the Worcestershire sauce. Taste and add salt if necessary. Stir and leave to stand in a cool place for an hour before serving.

Garganelli Romagna style *(serves 4)*

Pasta ingredients:
400 g (14 oz) white flour
4 tbsp. grated parmesan
  cheese
4 eggs
1 pinch nutmeg, salt

Sauce ingredients:
one 150 g (5½ oz) slice smoked
  streaky bacon
1 cup tomato sauce
  (or diluted tomato paste)
olive oil

Time needed: 1 hr. 30 min.

Garganelli are a typical dish from Romagna. To make them two utensils are essential; a "pettine" (a tool made from narrow strips of bamboo bound closely into wooden battens) and a smooth rod (you may find a smooth pencil ideal).

First make the dough: mix together the flour, eggs, salt, parmesan and pinch of nutmeg. Knead until smooth, then roll out thinly, flouring the pastry-board now and again. Using a sharp knife cut the dough into $3\frac{1}{2}$ cm ($1\frac{1}{2}$ inch)-sided squares and cover with a clean cloth to prevent the pasta drying out quickly.

Wrap the corner of each pasta square round the wooden rod and roll it up, pressing down on the "pettine". The result will be a type of maccheroni not unlike the "penne rigate" (grooved quills) commonly on sale in Italy. Take care to press firmly where the rolls join to seal and prevent their opening during cooking. Gently slide the "garganelli" off the rod, and place on the floured board while you finish the rest.

Begin to cook the garganelli in boiling salted water and in the meantime preparare the sauce. Heat up the tomato sauce in a pan. Dice the bacon and fry in a little oil. Drain the pasta when "al dente" and tip into the frying-pan with the bacon. Pour the boiling tomato sauce over the garganelli, stir for a moment over the heat and serve sprinkled with grated pecorino cheese (optional).

Garganelli can also be made with green pasta by adding spinach to the basic dough (see p. 26).

Gnocchetti (small gnocchi) made with pumpkin *(serves 4)*

Gnocchetti ingredients:
1 kg (2 lb) pumpkin
200 g (7 oz) white flour
1 egg
ground nutmeg
salt

Sauce ingredients:
home-made tomato sauce
   (or tomato purée)
a few tbsp. grated parmesan
   cheese
salt

Time needed: 2 hrs.

Peel the pumpkin and scrape out the seeds; cut it into large pieces and cook, either in the oven or in boiling salted water. Pulp it and place it in a bowl together with the sieved flour, egg, a pinch of salt and two generous pinches of nutmeg. Stir well, then heat up the tomato sauce.

Drop teaspoonsfuls of the mixture into a large saucepan of boiling salted water. Drain the gnocchetti with a skimmer or perforated spoon the moment they rise to the surface. Serve piping hot with the tomato sauce and the grated parmesan.

Gnocchetti (small gnocchi) in cotechino sauce *(serves 4)*

Gnocchetti ingredients:
330 g (11 oz) white flour
1 tbsp. chopped parsley
2 tbsp. grated parmesan
   cheese
nutmeg, salt

Sauce ingredients:
1 small cooked "cotechino"
   (a kind of spiced Italian
   sausage)
30 g (1 oz) butter
400 ml ($\frac{3}{4}$ pint) milk

Time needed: 1 hr.

Sieve 300 g (10 oz) flour into a bowl and add the parmesan, finely chopped parsley, pinches of salt and ground nutmeg and mix with enough water to obtain a rather thick dough.

Immerse teaspoonsfuls of the mixture into a large saucepan of boiling salted water, holding the spoon under the surface until the gnocchi comes off. Continue until all the mixture has been used up, resulting in small, irregularly shaped gnocchi. Boil them for 5 minutes, drain with a skimmer as they float to the surface and keep them warm.

Boil the milk. Melt the butter, preferably in an earthenware dish, sieve in the rest of the flour, mix, and gradually add the boiling milk, stirring all the time; cook the sauce over moderate heat, stirring with a wooden spoon until it turns creamy and smooth and is fully cooked. Add pinches of salt and ground

*Garganelli Romagna style (p. 66) and
Semolina gnocchi (p. 70)*

smooth and is fully cooked. Add pinches of salt and ground nutmeg, take off the heat and, using a fork, blend in the pieces of cotechino, skinned and crumbled. Dress the gnocchetti with the sauce, place in a shallow, ovenproof dish and brown in a hot oven (200°C/400°F/Gas 6) for 15 minutes. Serve hot.

Gnocchi di patate (Potato gnocchi) *(serves 4)*

Gnocchi ingredients:
1 kg (2 lb) baking potatoes
300 g (10 oz) plain white
 flour
1 egg
ground nutmeg, salt

Sauce ingredients:
home-made tomato sauce
 (or tinned tomatoes)
basil
grated parmesan cheese
salt

Time needed: 1 hr. 30 min.

Boil the potatoes in their skins, peel and mash them. Heap them on the pastry-board, adding generous pinches of salt and nutmeg, make a "crater", break in the egg and add a little of the flour. Begin to mix, gradually sieving in all the flour. The result should be a soft dough that does not stick to the fingers. Break off a piece of dough and roll it out on the floured pastry-board into a long, thin sausage. Chop this into 2 cm (1 inch)-long pieces and proceed in the same way until all the dough has been used up. Using your thumb, roll each piece gently over a grater or down the prongs of a fork.

Heat the tomato sauce and chopped basil (if using tinned tomatoes remember to strain them and remove the seeds). Cook the gnocchi in boiling salted water; drain them with a skimmer as they rise to the surface, dress them in a serving bowl with the hot tomato sauce and the parmesan cheese, mix gently and serve.

Gnocchi di semolino (Semolina gnocchi) *(serves 4)*

Gnocchi ingredients:
250 g (9 oz) semolina

50 g (2 oz) butter
50 g (2 oz) grated parmesan

3 egg-yolks
1 litre (2 pints) milk
ground nutmeg,
salt

Dressing ingredients:
70 g (2½ oz) butter
70 g (2½ oz) grated parmesan
   cheese

Time needed: 1 hr. 30 min.

Heat the milk in a saucepan with the butter and a few pinches of salt. As it comes to the boil sprinkle in the semolina and continue boiling over fairly low heat, stirring continuously with a wooden spoon until the mixture becomes quite thick and doughy, and starts coming away from the bottom and sides of the pan. Remove from the heat and add the yolks, one by one, a pinch of nutmeg, the parmesan. Beat vigorously to blend the ingredients well.

Pour the mixture onto a marble slab or other suitable smooth, well buttered worktop and spread it out with a metal spatula to a thickness of about 1 cm (½ inch). Dipping the spatula into boiling water now and again will help prevent the pasta sticking to it. Leave the paste to cool completely then cut it into 4 cm (1¾ inch)-circles using a pastry-cutter or the rim of a glass.

Place the semolina gnocchi in a well-greased, ovenproof dish, overlapping slightly, with little balls of left-over dough placed round the edge to decorate. Melt the remaining butter, pour over the gnocchi, sprinkle with grated parmesan and brown in an oven pre-heated to 180°C/350°F/Gas 4. Serve hot.

Lasagne with nut sauce *(serves 4)*

400 g (14 oz) home-made egg
   lasagne

Sauce ingredients:
100 g (3½ oz) shelled walnuts
50 g (2 oz) shelled, blanched
   almonds
100 g (3½ oz) butter

50 g (2 oz) white flour
a little cooking
   cream
¾ litre (1½ pints) milk
50 g (2 oz) grated parmesan
   cheese
pepper
salt

Time needed: 45 min.
(plus the time needed to prepare the lasagne)

Melt half the butter in a saucepan, sieve in the flour, stir well, and remove from the heat. Add a little warm milk, beating vigorously, then gradually add the rest of the milk, stirring gently. Replace the pan over the heat and boil the sauce for a few minutes, stirring all the time with a wooden spoon.
Remove from the heat and stir in the grated parmesan.
Finely chop the nuts, adding pinches of salt and pepper. Soften the remaining butter in another pan, adding a few tablespoons of warm cream and the chopped nuts.
Cook the lasagne in boiling salted water, drain when "al dente" and arrange in layers in an ovenproof dish, covering each layer with a little béchamel and a small amount of the nutty paste. Finish with a layer of béchamel and brown well in a hot oven pre-heated to 200°C/400°F/Gas 6. Serve hot.

Lasagne pie *(serves 4)*

400 g (14 oz) home-made
  egg lasagne

Sauce ingredients:
250 g (9 oz) tomato pulp
250 g (9 oz) minced beef
50 g (2 oz) rather fat Parma
  ham
20 g (1 oz) dried mushrooms
50 g (2 oz) butter
100 g (3½ oz) grated

parmesan cheese
3 tbsp. flour
1 small onion
1 small carrot
1 small stick celery
a pinch of chopped basil
  and parsley
½ glass red wine
½ litre (1 pint) milk
olive oil, nutmeg
pepper, salt

Time needed: 2 hrs. 30 min.

Soak the dried mushrooms in a little warm water.
To make the sauce, finely chop the Parma ham and fry it gently in a little olive oil. Chop the onion, carrot and celery, add to the

Gnocchi di patate (Potato gnocchi) (p. 70)

ham, and brown slightly before adding the meat and the mushrooms (softened, squeezed and chopped roughly). Cook for a few minutes, moisten with the red wine, add the chopped herbs, salt, pepper and a pinch of nutmeg. When the wine has evaporated, mix half a tablespoon of flour in a little water and add to the mixture; let it boil for a few seconds, then add the tomato pulp.

Thicken the sauce over moderate heat, stirring from time to time. To prepare the béchamel sauce melt the butter in a pan (keeping a little aside), sieve in the remaining flour, blend and stir in the boiling milk a little at a time. Add salt to taste and boil for a few minutes stirring all the time with a wooden spoon.

Cook the lasagne in boiling salted water, drain when "al dente" and lay on a clean tea-cloth to dry.

Grease an ovenproof dish and begin to layer meat sauce, pasta, more sauce, béchamel and a sprinkle of grated parmesan; then another layer of pasta and so on until all the ingredients have been used up. Ideally you should finish with a layer of pasta covered with béchamel. Cook in a hot oven (190°C/375°F/Gas 5) until the top is well browned and crispy.

Lasagnette caprice *(serves 4)*

400 g (14 oz) home-made egg lasagnette

Sauce ingredients:
100 g (3½ oz) cooked salame sausage
100 g (3½ oz) Bologna sausage

200 g (7 oz) boiled cauliflower tops
50 g (2 oz) butter
1 small mozzarella cheese
1 clove garlic
2 tbsp. grated parmesan
4 tbsp. olive oil
freshly ground pepper, salt

Time needed: 30 min.
(plus the time needed to prepare the lasagnette).

Cook the pasta in boiling salted water. Make the sauce while the pasta is cooking. Heat the butter and oil, add the clove of garlic (squashed gently with a fork), fry until golden brown and remove from the pan. Tip in the cauliflower pieces, sprinkle with a good pinch of freshly ground pepper and turn in the garlic-flavoured oil and butter for a few minutes. Add thinly-cut slices of Bologna sausage and salame and mix well. Drain the pasta when "al dente", tip it into the pan and sauté for a few minutes over high heat together with the cauliflower. Remove from the heat, sprinkle with the diced mozzarella and the parmesan, mix and serve.

Linguine with anchovy sauce *(serves 4)*

400 g (14 oz) home-made linguine

Sauce ingredients:
1 small bunch parsley

1 clove garlic
1 tube anchovy paste
4-5 tbsp. toasted bread crumbs
1 glass olive oil, salt

Time needed: 45 min.

Finely chop the clove of garlic and the parsley and fry gently in a pan with the olive oil. Add a squeeze of anchovy paste (the amount depends on your personal taste) and heat to dissolve (do not fry). Cook the linguine in salted boiling water, drain when "al dente", tip into a warmed serving bowl and dress with the anchovy sauce. Sprinkle with toasted bread-crumbs and serve.

Maccheroncini with artichoke sauce *(serves 4)*

400 g (14 oz) home-made ribbed maccheroncini

Sauce ingredients:
4 globe artichokes
80 g (3 oz) butter

3 tbsp. cooking cream
1 tbsp. finely chopped parsley
100 g (3½ oz) grated parmesan cheese
1 cup meat stock
pepper, salt

Time needed: 45 min.

Trim, wash and dry the artichokes (taking care to remove the tough outer leaves, thorny points and "strawy" centres). Slice thinly and simmer in half the butter, adding a tablespoon of broth from time to time. When cooked, season them with pinches of salt and freshly ground pepper. Cook the pasta in salted boiling water, drain when "al dente" and tip into the frying-pan with the artichokes, adding the remaining butter cut into pieces, 2 tablespoons of grated parmesan, the cream and the chopped parsley. Stir well over the heat, transfer into a wide serving bowl and serve immediately, sprinkled with the remaining parmesan.

Maccheroncini with mushroom sauce *(serves 4)*

400 g (14 oz) home-made maccheroncini

Sauce ingredients:
one 30 g (1 oz) slice smoked streaky bacon
400 g (14 oz) mushrooms

300 g (10 oz) tomatoes
½ onion
1 clove garlic
1 small bunch parsley
2 tbsp. dry white wine
4 tbsp. olive oil
salt, pepper

Time needed: 50 min.

Trim, wash, and slice the mushrooms. If using fresh tomatoes scald them in boiling water, drain, peel, remove the seeds and mash them with a fork (or strain, seed and mash the tinned variety). Finely chop the bacon, garlic and parsley and fry gently in the olive oil in an earthenware casserole; add the mushrooms when the mixture turns slightly golden brown. Stir, then pour in the wine and leave to evaporate. Add the tomato pulp, season with salt and pepper, and thicken over moderate heat, stirring occasionally. Cook the pasta in salted boiling water, drain when "al dente", dress with the sauce and serve immediately.

Maccheroncini with artichoke sauce (p. 75)

Maccheroncini alla cacciatora (in hunter's sauce) *(serves 4)*

400 g (14 oz) home-made
   maccheroncini

Sauce ingredients:
one $\frac{1}{2}$ inch-thick slice bacon
50 g (2 oz) slice Parma ham
20 g (1 oz) dried mushrooms
2 chicken livers
1 small onion

1 stick celery
1 clove garlic
1 bay leaf
2 tbsp. grated parmesan
   cheese
$\frac{1}{2}$ glass cooking cream
2 tbsp. brandy
5 tbsp. olive oil
freshly ground pepper, salt

Time needed: 1 hr.

Soak the dried mushrooms in warm water for 30 minutes.
Dice the bacon and ham. Finely chop the onion, garlic and celery and fry gently in the oil, preferably using an earthenware casserole. Clean, wash and chop the chicken livers and add to the mixture. Cook over high heat, stirring all the time. Season with salt and freshly ground pepper and douse with the brandy. Flambé, and as the flames die add the diced bacon and Parma ham, the bay leaf and the mushrooms (gently rinsed in their water) well squeezed and chopped. Stir the mixture and simmer over low heat for a further 15 minutes. Now pour in the cream, mixing well, and cook for another 10 minutes. Remove the bay leaf before serving.
Cook the maccheroncini in salted boiling water, drain when "al dente" and pour into a serving bowl. Dress with the hot sauce, stir, sprinkle with grated parmesan and serve.

Maccheroncini Puglia style *(serves 4)*

400 g (14 oz) home-made
   maccheroncini

Sauce ingredients:
1 kg (2 lb) cauliflower or

broccoli "tops"
120 g ($4\frac{1}{2}$ oz) bacon fat
4 tbsp. grated pecorino
   cheese
freshly ground pepper, salt

Time needed: 50 min.

Trim the cauliflower (or broccoli tops), wash and cook them in boiling salted water. When they are almost cooked add the pasta and cook them together in the same water.

Dice the bacon fat and fry it gently over low heat until it becomes almost transparent (do not brown).

Drain the pasta and the cauliflower (or broccoli) and tip into a large, previously warmed serving bowl. Dress with the diced bacon fat, sprinkle with grated pecorino and a good pinch of freshly ground pepper and serve.

Maccheroni baked in the oven *(serves 4)*

400 g (14 oz) ribbed
   maccheroni

Sauce ingredients:
500 g (1 lb) small ripe
   (or strained, tinned)
   tomatoes

1 bunch parsley
2 cloves garlic
1 bunch basil
3 tbsp. grated pecorino
   cheese
4 tbsp. olive oil
freshly ground pepper, salt

Time needed: 45 min.

If using fresh tomatoes, scald them in boiling water, drain and skin them.

Cut the tomatoes in half lengthwise, remove the seeds and place a single layer in a well-greased ovenproof dish.

Coarsely chop the garlic, parsley and basil, add to the tomatoes, season and douse with the remaining oil. Bake in a hot oven (180°C/350°F/Gas 4) for about 30 minutes.

During this time cook the maccheroni in salted water, drain when "al dente" and tip into the oven-dish containing the baked tomatoes, stir gently but thoroughly and bake for 5 minutes. Sprinkle with grated pecorino and serve straight away in the ovenproof dish.

Maccheroni Carmela fashion *(serves 4)*

400 g (14 oz) ribbed
  maccheroni

Sauce ingredients:
200 g (7 oz) minced pork
300 g (10 oz) tinned skinned
  tomatoes
50 g (2 oz) butter
50 g (2 oz) grated parmesan

2 globe artichokes
1 small mozzarella cheese
1 clove garlic
1 bunch of parsley and basil
1 small onion
½ glass dry white wine
1 pinch marjoram
2 tbsp. olive oil
freshly ground pepper, salt

Time needed: 1 hr.

Chop the garlic, onion, parsley, basil and marjoram. Wash and trim the artichokes, then slice them thinly; fry the chopped garlic, onion and herbs in the oil and butter using an earthenware casserole. Add the sliced artichokes and the minced pork and fry gently, stirring frequently with a wooden spoon. Season with salt and freshly ground pepper, douse with the wine and when this has evaporated add the sieved tomato pulp. Cook over moderate heat for 20 minutes, stirring from time to time.
Cook the maccheroni in salted boiling water, drain when "al dente", dress them with the meat sauce and tip them into an ovenproof dish. Cover the pasta with thin slices of mozzarella and grated parmesan and bake in a hot oven (190°C/375°F/Gas 5) for 10 minutes, then serve straight away.

Maccheroni with mascarpone sauce *(serves 4)*

400 g (14 oz) home-made
  ribbed maccheroni

Sauce ingredients:
100 g (3½ oz) mascarpone
  (or cream cheese)
100 g (3½ oz) butter

250 ml (8 fl oz) cooking
  cream
100 g (3½ oz) gruyère
  cheese
2 egg-yolks
freshly ground pepper
salt

Orecchiette with potatoes (p. 83)

Time needed: 30 min.

Shred the gruyère, melt the butter in a large frying-pan, add the cream and leave to thicken for a few minutes. Add the shredded gruyère and continue to cook over moderate heat, stirring until the cheese becomes tacky and pulls out into long threads.
Begin to cook the maccheroni in salted boiling water.
Soften the mascarpone (or cream cheese) in a bowl with a wooden spoon; add the egg-yolks, one at a time, and continue to beat until the mixture is smooth and creamy. Season with salt and pepper to taste.
Drain the pasta when "al dente", tip into the frying-pan and mix thoroughly with the cheese sauce for a few moments. Remove the pan from the heat and stir in the mascarpone, mixing vigorously. Serve while the cheese is still creamy and soft.

Maccheroni with greens *(serves 4)*

400 g (14 oz) home-made ribbed maccheroni	**½ litre (1 pint) milk**
	75 g (2½ oz) butter
	50 gr (2 oz) grated parmesan
Dressing ingredients:	**cheese**
300 g (10 oz) beet leaves or spring greens	**2 flat tbsp. white flour**
	ground nutmeg, salt

Time needed: 45 min.

Trim, wash, drain and cook the greens in a saucepan without adding further water (they will cook sufficiently in the water left on their leaves after washing). Add a little salt, drain when cooked, squeeze thoroughly, chop coarsely and keep warm.
Boil the milk. Make a béchamel sauce by melting 50 g (2 oz) butter in a pan, sieving in the flour and mixing with a wooden spoon to eliminate any lumps. Add the boiling milk, a little at a time, season with pinches of salt and nutmeg and cook over low heat for about 5 minutes, stirring all the time.
Cook the pasta in salted boiling water, drain, dress with the hot

béchamel, the warm greens, grated parmesan and knobs of the remaining butter. Stir delicately and serve.

Maccheroni tossed in the frying-pan *(serves 4)*

350 g (12 oz) home-made
   ribbed maccheroni

Sauce ingredients:
   500 g (1 lb) tinned skinned
   tomatoes
50 g (2 oz) grated parmesan

3 eggs
1 small onion
1 bunch basil
1 medium-sized mozzarella
   cheese
olive oil
freshly ground pepper, salt

Time needed: 1 hr.

Finely chop the onion and sweat it in a few tablespoons of olive oil over low heat using an earthenware casserole. Add the sieved tomatoes, the bunch of basil, and season. Simmer over low heat.
Begin cooking the pasta in salted boiling water. Beat the eggs, seasoning them, and cut the mozzarella into small pieces.
When the sauce is cooked, and quite thick, remove the bunch of basil and pour the rest of the sauce into a frying-pan, add the mozzarella pieces and place the pan over low heat.
Drain the pasta, tip it into the frying-pan, cover with the beaten eggs and grated parmesan, then stir gently with a wooden fork until the mozzarella melts. Remove from the heat and serve.

Orecchiette with potatoes *(serves 4)*

Pasta ingredients:
350 g (12 oz) white flour
100 g (3½ oz) durum wheat
   semolina

Dressing ingredients:
4 medium-sized potatoes

a few sprigs fresh rue
   (or a few leaves
   fresh basil)
fresh tomato sauce
130 g (4½ oz) grated pecorino
   cheese
salt

Time needed: 1 hr. 30 min.

This is another traditional dish from Puglia; "orecchiette" literally means "little ears".

Mix the two flours on the pastry-board, adding a pinch of salt; make a "crater" and add enough tepid water to make the dough. Knead for a good 10 minutes until little bubbles begin to appear. The dough should be rather firm, a little stiffer than bread dough (rather like that used for "Cavatieddi", see page 52). Pull off a piece of dough and roll it out on a well-floured pastry-board into a long, pencil-thin sausage.

Cut this into 1 cm (½ inch) lengths and using a blunt-ended knife or a round-ended fork handle, press and slightly drag each piece on the board. This deft action (done at top speed by the Puglian housewives) gives the pasta a shell-like shape, which must then be fitted on the tip of your thumb and turned inside-out, if necessary with the aid of a knife. Continue in this way until all the dough has been used up. Leave the orecchiette on the floured board, not touching one another, to dry until the following day — no longer, or they tend to break up when cooked.

Boil a generous amount of salted water and tip in first the peeled, diced potatoes, then the sprigs of rue or basil and lastly the orecchiette. When cooked, drain all the ingredients, remove the herbs, and tip the pasta and potatoes into a large serving dish, adding warmed tomato sauce and a generous sprinkle of grated pecorino cheese. Serve immediately.

Orecchiette with sweet-turnip tops *(serves 4)*

300 g (10 oz) home-made
  orecchiette

Dressing ingredients:
600 g (1¼ lb) sweet-

turnip tops
4 anchovy fillets
1 clove garlic
4 tbsp. olive oil
salt

Time needed: 45 min.

Paglia e fieno with mushroom sauce (p. 86)

Trim the sweet-turnip tops; separate the flowered tops from the leaves and stalks, wash all the pieces and shake off the excess water. Boil a generous amount of salted water and drop in first the leaves and stalks cut into pieces; wait a few minutes, then add the pasta. When the latter is half-cooked add the flowered tops. Drain the ingredients well when the pasta is "al dente"; squeeze the greens with a fork to eliminate as much water as possible.

Finely chop the clove of garlic and the anchovies and fry gently in the olive oil using a large frying-pan. Add the pasta and the greens, mix the ingredients gently over low heat for a few minutes, then serve hot.

Paglia e fieno (straw and hay) with mushroom sauce *(serves 4)*

200 g (7 oz) home-made
   egg tagliolini
200 g (7 oz) home-made
   green tagliolini

Sauce ingredients:
300 g (10 oz) mushrooms

100 g ($3^{1}\!/_2$ oz) butter
1 clove garlic
2 tbsp. chopped parsley
2 tbsp. grated parmesan
   cheese
2 tbsp. olive oil
pepper, salt

Time needed: 40 min.

Clean the mushrooms meticulously and slice them (not too thinly). Fry the clove of garlic, squashed firmly with a fork, in the olive oil. Remove it as it turns golden brown and add the mushrooms to the garlic-flavoured oil; season with salt and pepper and cook for 15 minutes over moderate heat. Do not cover. During this time cook the tagliolini in a generous amount of salted boiling water. When the mushrooms are cooked, sprinkle them with the chopped parsley, stir and remove from the heat.

Melt the butter in a large frying-pan. Drain the tagliolini when "al dente", tip into the frying-pan, add the mushrooms and sauté for a few moments. Stir through, then pour the pasta into a serving bowl, sprinkle with the parmesan and serve at once.

Paglia e fieno with fresh tomatoes and basil *(serves 4)*

200 g (7 oz) home-made egg
  tagliatelline
200 g (7 oz) home-made
  green tagliatelline

Sauce ingredients:
500 g (1 lb) ripe tomatoes
1 bunch fresh basil
olive oil, pepper, salt

Time needed: 1 hr.

This dish is particularly appreciated during the summer months. Scald the tomatoes for a few moments in boiling water, drain, skin, remove the seeds and cut the pulp into strips. Salt and leave the tomato to drip in a colander (this eliminates part of its high water content).
Wash the basil leaves gently but thoroughly, and chop finely.
Boil the pasta in salted water, drain when "al dente", add the tomato strips, the basil, 4 or 5 tablespoons of olive oil and a good pinch of freshly ground pepper. Serve straight away.

"Palline" (small balls) of spinach and ricotta *(serves 4)*

Ingredients:
1 kg (2 lb) spinach
500 g (1 lb) ricotta cheese
100 g (3½ oz) grated
  parmesan cheese
3 or 4 egg-yolks

70 g (2½ oz) butter
50 g (1 oz) margarine
80 g (3 oz) white
  flour
nutmeg
salt

Time needed: 2 hrs.

Trim, wash and boil the spinach, adding a pinch of salt and stirring it gently in a pan with a wooden spoon using only the water left on the leaves after washing. Drain, squeeze dry and chop finely, then pour it into a bowl and add the ricotta cheese, already beaten and softened with a fork. Add the egg-yolks, one at a time (should the ricotta seem too thick use the fourth yolk too), season with salt and nutmeg and finally add 50 g (2 oz) of grated parmesan. Sieve in the flour, little by little, stirring well to blend into a fairly firm dough. Grease your hands and roll out small gnocchetti (shaped like small rugby balls) with the dough, placing them on a floured plate as you make them (not touching one another).

Drop them gently into salted boiling water for about 3 minutes. Drain them with a skimmer as they float to the surface and layer them in a wide serving bowl, dressing each layer with a mixture of melted butter and margarine. Top with the rest of the grated parmesan and serve hot.

Pappardelle delight *(serves 4)*

400 g (14 oz) home-made
  pappardelle

Sauce ingredients:
100 g (3½ oz) smoked ham
100 g (3½ oz) shelled peas
50 g (2 oz) butter
20 g (1 oz) dried mushrooms

2 eggs
1 small handful parsley
1 small onion
1 clove garlic
1 piece hot red pepper
2 tbsp. grated pecorino cheese
a little cooking cream
olive oil, salt, pepper

Time needed: 1 hr. 30 min.

Soak the mushrooms in a little warm water.

Melt half the butter in a casserole, add the peas, salt and cook, adding a tablespoon of water from time to time.

Dice the ham and brown gently in a saucepan with 2 tablespoons of olive oil; add the hot red pepper and keep over the heat for another few moments.

Finely chop the onion, the garlic and the parsley and fry them together in the rest of the butter using another pan. Rinse the mushrooms in the water used to soak them, squeeze and chop them coarsely. Season with salt and pepper and cook over low heat, stirring now and again.

Beat the eggs, cream and pecorino together in a large bowl.

Penne all'arrabbiata (in "infuriated" sauce!) (p. 90)

Cook the pappardelle in salted boiling water, drain and tip into the bowl, mixing energetically. Add the ham, the mushrooms in their sauce together with the peas, mix well and serve hot.

Penne alla pecorara (Penne in shepherd's sauce) *(serves 4)*

400 g (14 oz) home-made
  penne rigate

Dressing ingredients:
120 g (4½ oz) diced smoked
  bacon
30 g (1 oz) butter

30 g (1 oz) grated parmesan
  cheese
30 g (1 oz) grated pecorino
  cheese
200 ml (6 fl oz) cooking cream
1 tbsp. fresh, chopped basil
black pepper, salt

Time needed: 30 min.

Cook the pasta in plenty of boiling salted water.
Make the dressing by browning the diced bacon in the butter and beating the two grated cheeses in a bowl together with the cream.
Drain the penne when "al dente", tip them into the bowl containing the creamy cheese mixture, top with the diced bacon and its hot oil and mix well. Sprinkle generously with freshly ground black pepper and the chopped basil and serve immediately.

Penne all'arrabbiata (Penne in "infuriated" sauce!) *(serves 4)*

400 g (14 oz) penne rigate

Sauce ingredients:
150 g (5½ oz) lean bacon
200 g (7 oz) boletus
  mushrooms
400 g (14 oz) small, ripe
  tomatoes (or tinned

  skinned tomatoes)
40 g (1½ oz) butter
50 g (2 oz) grated pecorino
  cheese
1 hot red pepper
1 sprig basil
1 clove garlic
olive oil, salt

Time needed: 50 min.

Clean, wash and slice the mushrooms thinly.

Fry the bacon, cut into strips, in an earthenware casserole with a little oil and half the butter. The moment the bacon turns golden brown and crispy, lift it out onto a plate and set it aside.

Over low heat, squash the garlic firmly with a fork in the oil left after browning the bacon and remove it as it begins to turn golden brown. Now pour the mushrooms into the same casserole and cook over high heat, stirring frequently. Two minutes before removing them from the heat add a little salt and the bacon.

Skin the tomatoes (if using fresh ones, scald them first for a few minutes in boiling water) and remove the seeds.

Mash the tomatoes and tip the pulp into another saucepan with the basil, the chopped hot pepper and salt to taste. Cook over low heat to thicken the sauce.

At this point add the mushrooms and bacon and keep the whole mixture over the heat for a further two minutes.

At the same time cook the penne in a generous amount of boiling salted water, drain when "al dente" and dress with the hot sauce, the rest of the butter cut into small knobs, and top with the grated pecorino. Serve straight away.

Penne in vodka sauce *(serves 4)*

400 g (14 oz) penne lisce	1 hot red pepper
	3 tbsp. tomato paste
Sauce ingredients:	1 small glass vodka
50 g (2 oz) butter	200 ml (6 fl oz) cooking
50 g (2 oz) grated parmesan	cream
cheese	1 tbsp. brandy

Time needed: 30 min.

Cook the penne in plenty of salted boiling water. Meanwhile, melt the butter in a large pan over low heat, add the hot red

pepper and the tomato paste; let the flavours blend, then add the cream and as soon as the sauce comes to the boil pour in the vodka and the brandy. Remove the red pepper and stir in the parmesan. Drain the pasta when "al dente", tip it into the pan, stir it into the sauce and leave over very low heat for 2 minutes before serving.

Penne with salame *(serves 4)*

400 g (14 oz) penne rigate

Sauce ingredients:
200 g (7 oz) salame, cut into thickish strips
40 g (1½ oz) butter

50 g (2 oz) grated parmesan cheese
1 sprig rosemary
2 eggs
½ glass dry white wine
olive oil, pepper, salt

Time needed: 30 min.

Begin to cook the pasta in plenty of salted boiling water.
Meanwhile, brown the salame strips in a casserole with the butter, a little oil and the sprig of rosemary. Douse with the wine, allow it to evaporate and turn off the heat.
Beat the eggs in a large bowl together with the grated parmesan and pinches of salt and pepper. Drain the penne when "al dente", and tip them into a bowl containing the eggs and cheese. Mix and add the salame and its oily residue. Remove the rosemary and serve immediately, topping each helping with more grated parmesan.

Penne al telefono (Penne "on the phone") *(serves 4)*

400 g (14 oz) penne rigate

Sauce ingredients:
100 g (3½ oz) boiled ham (cut in a 1 cm (½ inch)-thick slice)

50 g (2 oz) butter
50 g (2 oz) white flour
1 mozzarella cheese
½ litre (1 pint) milk
nutmeg, salt

Time needed: 45 min.

First make the béchamel; boil the milk, melt the butter in another pan and gradually sieve in the flour, stirring all the time with a wooden spoon to dissolve any lumps. Add the boiling milk, a little at a time, stirring continuously. Add salt to taste and boil over low heat for 10 minutes, mixing slowly all the time. Remove from the heat and add a pinch of nutmeg.
Cook the penne in salted boiling water. Dice the mozzarella and tip the pieces into a bowl together with the ham (cut into strips) and the béchamel. Drain the pasta when "al dente", pour into the bowl containing the sauce, mix well and serve.

Penne baked in ragù *(serves 4)*

400 g (14 oz) penne rigate

Sauce ingredients:
100 g (3½ oz) lean minced
   beef
400 g (14 oz) fresh, ripe (or
   tinned, skinned) tomatoes

60 g (2¼ oz) butter
50 g (2 oz) grated parmesan
   cheese
1 small piece onion
1 sprig basil
2 tbsp. olive oil
salt

Time needed: 1 hr. 30 min.

Finely chop the onion and sweat it in a casserole with the oil and 40 g (1½ oz) butter. Cook for 2 minutes and add the minced beef; stir to blend the ingredients, then add the basil leaves (cleaned) and the tomatoes (with their seeds removed and chopped coarsely), and leave the ragù to cook for at least one hour over moderate heat, stirring occasionally. Boil the penne in salted water for 7 to 8 minutes, drain and arrange them in layers in a greased ovenproof dish, covering each layer with a little ragù and a sprinkle of parmesan (you should finish with a layer of ragù). Bake in an oven pre-heated to 180 °C/350 °F/Gas 4 for 15 minutes, remove and serve in the ovenproof dish.

Penne baked with sardines *(serves 4)*

250 g (9 oz) penne	250 ml (8 fl oz) milk
	2 tbsp. bread-crumbs
Sauce ingredients:	1 small glass cooking cream
120 g (4½ oz) butter	3 tbsp. grated parmesan
50 g (2 oz) white flour	1 tbsp. finely chopped
12 fresh (or tinned) sardines	parsley
4 fresh, ripe tomatoes	pepper, salt

Time needed: 1 hr.

Cook the penne in plenty of salted boiling water for 10 minutes; drain and pass briefly under cold running water to halt the cooking process. Boil the milk. Melt 50 g (2 oz) butter in a casserole, sieve in the flour, stirring with a wooden spoon, and add the boiling milk a little at a time, stirring continuously. Cook over low heat, still stirring, until the béchamel becomes soft and smooth, season and stir in the cream and half the parmesan. Toss the penne with this sauce, grease an ovenproof dish, sprinkle in the bread-crumbs and tip in the pasta.

Fillet the sardines, wash them thoroughly, dry them and lay them over the pasta (if using the tinned variety, drain off the oil). Top with the segmented tomatoes, adding pinches of salt and pepper and sprinkling with the remaining parmesan. Melt the rest of the butter and pour it over the ingredients. Bake in an oven pre-heated to 180°C/350°F/Gas 4 for 20 minutes. Remove from the oven, top with the chopped parsley and serve piping hot.

Penne in pepper sauce *(serves 4)*

400 g (14 oz) penne rigate	20 g (1 oz) capers
	1 small bunch basil
Sauce ingredients:	2 large yellow peppers
300 g (10 oz) fresh, ripe	1 small onion
tomatoes (or tinned tomatoes)	1 tbsp. olive oil
100 g (3½ oz) pitted olives	1 pinch oregano
80 g (3 oz) butter	salt, pepper

Wash the peppers, remove the seeds and stringy insides and cut into thin strips. Scald the fresh tomatoes in boiling water, then drain and skin them. Remove the seeds and cut the tomatoes into thin segments (tinned tomatoes should be strained, their seeds removed).

Fry the finely chopped onion in oil in a casserole. Add the peppers and tomatoes, season and cook over moderate heat, stirring occasionally. Sieve the sauce, then add the capers, olives, chopped basil and oregano. Boil the penne in plenty of salted water and drain when "al dente".

Melt the butter in a large frying-pan, tip in the pasta and sauté over high heat for 2 minutes, stirring with a wooden spoon. Add the sauce, mix again and serve immediately.

Pennette with asparagus *(serves 4)*

400 g (14 oz) pennette rigate	**50 g (2 oz) grated parmesan cheese**
Sauce ingredients:	**a little cooking cream**
500 g (1 lb) asparagus	**olive oil**
20 g (1 oz) butter	**pepper, salt**

Time needed: 50 min.

Trim away the hard part of the asparagus stalks, wash them and steam them (or cook in very little salted water). Drain well, shaking off the excess water, and chop finely. Melt the butter with a few tablespoons of olive oil in an earthenware casserole, add the asparagus, salt and pepper to taste, and brown gently.

Cook the pasta in a good quantity of salted boiling water.

Stir about 200 ml (6 fl oz) of cooking cream into the asparagus mixture and boil for a few minutes. Drain the pasta when "al dente", dress it with the asparagus sauce, sprinkle with the grated parmesan and a dash of freshly ground pepper and serve.

Ravioli with ragù (p. 99) and Pizzoccheri (p. 98)

Pizzoccheri *(serves 4)*

Pasta ingredients:
300 g (10 oz) buckwheat
   flour
100 g (3½ oz) plain white
   flour
1 egg, a little milk, salt

Sauce ingredients:
100 g (3½ oz) butter

200 g (7 oz) bitto (cheese
   from Valtellina)
   or fontina cheese
3 or 4 medium-sized potatoes
1 small cabbage
a few sage leaves
1 clove garlic
pepper
salt

Time needed: about 2 hrs.

This is a typical dish from Valtellina.

Mix the buckwheat flour and the white flour together on the pastry-board; make a "crater" in the centre and break in the egg; add a pinch of salt and a drop of milk. Mix and add enough water to make a smooth, firm dough. Knead energetically for a few moments until the dough is nice and smooth. Roll it out into a thickish sheet, then cut it into 1 cm (½ inch)-wide strips. Now divide the strips into 5 to 6 cm (2-2½ inch) lengths.

Trim the cabbage, selecting the best leaves, wash, drain and shred them.

Boil a generous amount of salted water. Peel and dice the potatoes, then drop them into the boiling water together with the cabbage. When the cabbage is half cooked add the pasta. Cook thoroughly, stirring occasionally with a wooden fork or spoon.

While the pasta and vegetables are cooking, melt the butter with the whole clove of garlic in a pan with the sage leaves and leave them to fry gently.

Cut the bitto cheese or fontina cheese into slices sufficiently thin to melt over the heat.

Drain the pasta and vegetables and arrange them in layers in a wooden bowl, topping each layer with slices of cheese, pepper and tiny pieces of butter. Mix and serve hot.

Ravioli with ragù (meat sauce) *(serves 4)*

Pasta ingredients:
a sheet of dough made from
   400 g (14 oz) white flour
   and 4 eggs

Filling ingredients:
300 g (10 oz) minced veal
30 g (1 oz) butter
50 g (2 oz) Parma ham
150 g (5½ oz) salsiccia (spiced
   Italian sausage)
one 100 g (3½ oz) slice
   Bologna sausage
30 g (1 oz) grated parmesan
1 egg
1 tsp. beef extract
1 small onion

dry white wine
2 tbsp. olive oil
nutmeg, pepper, salt

Sauce ingredients:
200 g (7 oz) minced beef
400 g (14 oz) tomato pulp
20 g (¾ oz) bacon
20 g (¾ oz) dried mushrooms
75 g (2½ oz) grated parmesan
1 small onion
1 stick celery
1 clove garlic
1 bay leaf
1 clove
red wine
olive oil, salt, pepper

Time needed: about 2 hrs.

Soak the mushrooms for 30 minutes in tepid water.
To prepare the meat sauce (ragù), gently fry the chopped bacon, celery, onion and garlic in a casserole with a few tablespoons of oil. Add the meat, season and mix well. Add the bay leaf, clove and mushrooms (squeezed and chopped). After a few minutes sprinkle with half a glass of red wine and let it evaporate. Add the strained tomato pulp and continue cooking over low heat, stirring occasionally. To make the filling, fry the chopped onion, Bologna sausage and Parma ham in the butter and 2 tablespoons of oil. Add the meat and sausage and brown well. Douse with half a glass of white wine, allow to evaporate and add the beef extract diluted in a little warm water, salt, pepper and cook until the mixture thickens. Remove from the heat, add the parmesan and, after 2 minutes, the egg and a pinch of nutmeg. Make the ravioli with the dough and filling following the instructions on p. 15. Cook the ravioli in plenty of salted

boiling water, drain and dress them in layers with the meat sauce and the grated parmesan.

Ravioli with fish and herbs *(serves 4)*

Pasta ingredients:
a sheet of dough made from
  400 g (14 oz) white flour
  and 2 eggs

100 g (3½ oz) ricotta cheese
1-2 eggs
70 g (2½ oz) grated parmesan
salt, pepper

Filling ingredients:
300 g (10 oz) baked or
  steamed fish
500 g (1 lb) borage or beet
  leaves (or spinach)

Dressing ingredients:
chopped parsley, garlic,
  basil, onion, thyme and
  marjoram
30 g (1 oz) butter, a little oil

Time needed: 2 hrs.

For the filling, wash, boil, squeeze and chop the greens. Skin, bone and mash the fish, then mix with the greens. Add the ricotta, the grated parmesan, the eggs (just enough for a firm consistency), season and mix well. Prepare the ravioli (see p. 15) and boil them in plenty of salted water. Fry the chopped herbs in two tablespoons of oil and the butter over low heat until the herbs wilt. Drain the ravioli, tip them into a serving bowl, dress them in layers with the aromatic sauce and serve immediately.

Rigatoni country style *(serves 4)*

400 g (14 oz) rigatoni

Sauce ingredients:
50 g (2 oz) fat bacon
80 g (3 oz) lean Parma ham
1 small onion
1 stick celery

1 small bunch basil
1 clove garlic
1 handful parsley
grated parmesan cheese
3 tbsp. olive oil
black pepper in grains
salt

Rigatoni with mortadella (p. 102)

101

Time needed: 40 min.

Finely chop the fat bacon, onion, celery, parsley, basil and garlic and fry gently in an earthenware casserole with the oil. As the ingredients begin to turn slightly golden, add the diced Parma ham, stir and leave to simmer over low heat.

In the meantime, cook the rigatoni in a generous amount of boiling salted water, drain them when "al dente" and tip them into a bowl; sprinkle them with a little freshly ground black pepper and dress with the sauce. Mix carefully and serve them topped with a good sprinkle of grated parmesan.

Rigatoni with mortadella (Bologna sausage) *(serves 4)*

400 g (14 oz) rigatoni

Dressing ingredients:
100 g (3½ oz) Bologna

sausage cut into strips
30 g (1 oz) butter
50 g (2 oz) bread-crumbs
pepper, salt

Time needed: 30 min.

Boil the rigatoni in plenty of salted water. Whilst they are cooking, melt the butter in a large pan, add the strips of Bologna sausage and the bread-crumbs and fry gently for 2 minutes.

Drain the rigatoni when "al dente", tip them into the pan and mix them with the Bologna sausage and bread-crumbs over moderate heat for a few moments. Put salt and pepper to taste, pour into a large bowl and serve straight away.

Rigatoni Norcia style *(serves 4)*

400 g (14 oz) rigatoni

Sauce ingredients:
50 g (2 oz) butter
20 g (1 oz) margarine

1 spicy Italian pork sausage
2 tbsp. white flour
grated parmesan cheese
½ litre (1 pint) milk
salt

Time needed: 1 hr.

Boil the milk and in the meantime skin and chop the sausage, then brown it gently in the margarine.

Melt the butter in a pan, sieve in the flour (stirring with a wooden spoon to eliminate any lumps), then gradually add the boiling milk, stirring all the time. Cook over moderate heat for 10 minutes, stirring continuously.

Cook the rigatoni in a generous amount of boiling salted water, drain them when "al dente", dress them with the hot sauce and the sausage, add a generous sprinkle of grated parmesan and serve immediately.

Rigatoni tossed in cream *(serves 4)*

400 g (14 oz) rigatoni	**1 clove garlic**
	4 basil leaves
Sauce ingredients:	**2 tbsp. grated parmesan**
300 g (10 oz) tinned, skinned	**cheese**
tomatoes	**1 tbsp. soya sauce**
50 g (2 oz) butter	**200 ml (6 fl oz) cooking cream**
1 small onion	**2 tbsp. olive oil**
1 stick celery	**freshly ground pepper, salt**

Time needed: 45 min.

Finely chop the onion, garlic and celery and sweat in the oil and butter over low heat, using an earthenware casserole. As the ingredients begin to turn slightly golden, add the strained, sieved tomatoes and the basil leaves, and salt if necessary. Thicken the sauce over moderate heat and stir in the cream and soya sauce as it becomes denser. Stir well and leave to simmer slowly.

Cook the rigatoni in a generous amount of boiling salted water; drain when "al dente", tip into a large serving bowl and dress with the sauce and the grated parmesan. Top with a good pinch of freshly ground pepper, mix gently and serve immediately.

Rigatoni with mushroom and sausage sauce *(serves 4)*

400 g (14 oz) rigatoni

Sauce ingredients:
300 g (10 oz) mushrooms
200 (7 oz) spiced
  Italian sausage
300 g (10 oz) tomato pulp
50 g (2 oz) butter

80 g (3 oz) grated parmesan
  cheese
a little stock
1 onion
1 carrot
1 bay leaf
fresh marjoram
olive oil, pepper, salt

Time needed: 1 hr.

Clean and slice the mushrooms. Finely chop the onion and carrot and fry gently in the butter and 2 to 3 tablespoons of olive oil. Add the bay leaf, the sliced sausage and the mushrooms and brown all the ingredients slowly. Add the sieved tomato pulp, salt, pepper and mix, then douse with a few tablespoons of stock. Cover and thicken over moderate heat. Before removing from the heat, sprinkle in a tablespoon of finely chopped marjoram.
Fifteen minutes before taking the sauce off the heat, throw the rigatoni into plenty of boiling salted water, drain when "al dente" and toss in a bowl with the hot sauce and grated parmesan.

Rigatoni with ricotta and salame *(serves 4)*

400 g (14 oz) rigatoni

Sauce ingredients:
200 g (7 oz) ricotta cheese
60 g (2¼ oz) diced raw salame
30 g (1 oz) butter

2 tbsp. grated parmesan
  cheese
3 sage leaves
200 ml (6 fl oz) cooking
  cream
freshly ground pepper, salt

Time needed: 40 min.

Using a fork, force the ricotta through a sieve into a bowl, add the parmesan, a pinch of pepper and salt and mix thoroughly.

Put the rigatoni on to cook in plenty of boiling water.

Brown the butter in a pan, adding the diced salame and the sage leaves; leave over the heat for a few minutes, then remove the sage leaves and tip the salame into the bowl containing the ricotta. Stir in the cream and 2 tablespoons of the water being used to cook the pasta.

Drain the rigatoni when "al dente", tip them into the bowl with the ricotta and salame, mix well and serve straight away.

Spaghetti with garlic, oil and hot pepper *(serves 4)*

400 g (14 oz) spaghetti	**2 cloves garlic**
	5 tbsp. olive oil
Dressing ingredients:	**20 g (1 oz) butter**
1 chilli pepper	**salt**

Time needed: 30 min.

Boil the spaghetti in plenty of salted water.

Make the dressing while the pasta is cooking. Peel the cloves of garlic, add them together with the chilli pepper to the hot oil and fry gently over low heat until the garlic turns a deep golden brown. Remove both the garlic and the hot pepper.

Drain the spaghetti when "al dente", tip it into a serving bowl and toss quickly with the hot oil and butter. Serve straight away.

Spaghetti alla carbonara *(serves 4)*

400 g (14 oz) spaghetti	**3 eggs**
(or bucatini)	**3 tbsp. grated pecorino (or**
	parmesan) cheese
Sauce ingredients:	**4 tbsp. olive oil**
100 g (3½ oz) salted pork or	**3-4 tbsp. cooking cream**
smoked streaky bacon	**freshly ground pepper, salt**

Time needed: 30 min.

Begin to cook the spaghetti in an abundant amount of boiling water, then concentrate on making the dressing.

Gently fry the diced bacon in a pan with the olive oil. Break the eggs into a large bowl and beat them, adding half the grated cheese and a generous pinch of pepper (and, if you wish, 3 to 4 tablespoons of cream). Drain the spaghetti when "al dente", tip into the bowl and mix vigorously to prevent the eggs from coagulating. Heat up the bacon and oil again and add to the spaghetti and eggs. Mix thoroughly and serve straight away, very hot, sprinkling each helping with more grated cheese.

Spaghetti alla carrettiera (in carter's sauce) *(serves 4)*

400 g (14 oz) spaghetti

Sauce ingredients:
70 g (2½ oz) salted pork or smoked streaky bacon
70 g (2½ oz) tinned tuna in oil

200 g (7 oz) fresh boletus mushrooms, (or 20 g (1 oz) dried mushrooms)
½ tbsp. meat extract
1 clove garlic
3 tbsp. olive oil
freshly ground pepper, salt

Time needed: 45 min.

Clean and thinly slice the mushrooms; if using the dried variety, soak for 15 minutes in tepid water, squeeze and chop coarsely. Cut the salted pork or bacon into thin strips and fry gently in a casserole with the olive oil and the clove of garlic, squashing the latter firmly with a fork. When the fatty part of the salted pork or bacon becomes transparent, remove the garlic, add the mushrooms and cook over low heat, gradually adding the meat extract diluted in a little boiling water. Salt to taste (if necessary), add a pinch of freshly ground pepper and, just before removing the pan from the heat, add the tuna, mashed coarsely with a fork. Mix thoroughly.

Boil the spaghetti in plenty of salted water, drain when "al dente" and toss in a bowl with the hot sauce. Serve at once.

Spaghetti alla meridionale (southern Italian style) *(serves 4)*

400 g (14 oz) spaghetti

Sauce ingredients:
180 g (6½ oz) tomato pulp
50 g (2 oz) large black,
    pitted olives
15 g (½ oz) small
    capers

4 anchovy fillets
2 pickled gherkins
2 cloves garlic
1 tbsp. chopped basil
1 pinch oregano
100 ml (3 fl oz) olive oil
pepper
salt

Time needed: 30 min.

Chop the anchovies and gherkins, then slice the olives.
Brown the garlic in the oil, using an earthenware casserole; add a dash of pepper, the chopped anchovies and gherkins, the capers and chopped olives. Add the strained, chopped tomato pulp, salt to taste and cook for about 15 minutes.
Meanwhile, cook the spaghetti in a generous amount of salted boiling water and drain when "al dente". Just before removing the sauce from the heat, sprinkle in the basil and oregano. Now pour it over the spaghetti in a bowl, mix well and serve immediately.

Spaghetti Spoleto style *(serves 4)*

400 g (14 oz) spaghetti

Sauce ingredients:
180 g (6½ oz) diced smoked
    streaky bacon
300 g (10 oz) fresh ripe
    tomatoes

2 medium-sized onions
3 tbsp. olive oil
3 tbsp. grated pecorino (or
    parmesan) cheese
fresh marjoram
freshly ground black pepper
salt

Time needed: 40 min.

Finely chop the onions and place in an earthenware casserole

Spaghetti alla carbonara (p. 106)

with the olive oil; add the diced bacon and fry gently, stirring continuously with a wooden spoon. After about 10 minutes add the tomatoes (washed and cut into pieces). Cook the sauce over moderately high heat and at the last moment salt to taste, add a dash of freshly ground pepper and the chopped marjoram.

Boil the spaghetti in plenty of salted water, drain when "al dente" and tip into a serving bowl. Toss with the sauce, sprinkle with the grated pecorino, stir through and serve immediately.

Spaghetti alla puttanesca (in harlot's sauce) *(serves 4)*

400 g (14 oz) spaghetti	1 handful chopped parsley
	2 cloves garlic
Sauce ingredients:	1 tbsp. capers
100 g (3½ oz) black olives	4 ripe tomatoes
40 g (1½ oz) butter	2 tbsp. olive oil
4 anchovy fillets (unsalted)	pepper, salt

Time needed: 30 min.

Brown the sliced garlic in a pan with the oil and butter; chop and add the anchovies. Fry gently and add the capers, olives and tomatoes (skinned and shredded). Cook for about 15 minutes, stirring occasionally. When the sauce is almost done, taste and add salt and pepper if necessary. Boil the spaghetti in plenty of salted water, drain when slightly "al dente", toss in a serving bowl with the hot sauce, sprinkle with the parsley and serve.

Spaghetti alla stallina (in stable-hand's sauce) *(serves 4)*

400 g (14 oz) spaghetti	2 cloves garlic
	2 tbsp. grated pecorino
Sauce ingredients:	(or parmesan) cheese
150 g (5½ oz) lean smoked	3 tbsp. olive oil
bacon (cut in one thick	freshly ground pepper
slice)	salt

Time needed: 30 min.

Boil a generous amount of salted water and throw in the spaghetti. While this is cooking prepare the sauce. Slice the bacon into strips; heat up the oil in a large frying-pan, add the chopped garlic and the bacon and fry gently over low heat until the bacon fat turns transparent. Drain the spaghetti when only half cooked and tip into the frying-pan to finish cooking, stirring frequently. Just before removing the pasta from the heat, sprinkle with the grated cheese and a dash of freshly ground pepper.

Spaghetti with peanut sauce *(serves 4)*

400 g (14 oz) spaghetti

Sauce ingredients:
60 g (2¼ oz) peanuts

4 unsalted anchovy fillets
60 g (2¼ oz) butter
1 piece chilli pepper
olive oil, salt

Time needed: 40 min.

Begin to boil the spaghetti in plenty of salted water.
Make the sauce while the pasta is cooking. Heat the butter and a little oil in a large frying-pan. Add the hot pepper and chopped anchovies and fry gently over low heat; add the shelled, peeled, coarsely pounded peanuts and brown them, stirring frequently.
Drain the spaghetti when "al dente", tip into the frying-pan and blend the ingredients over the heat for a few minutes. Pour into a warmed bowl and serve immediately.

Spaghetti with onion sauce *(serves 4)*

400 g (14 oz) spaghetti

Sauce ingredients:
500 g (1 lb) sweet onions
30 g (1 oz) butter

2 tbsp. grated parmesan
1 small bunch parsley
½ glass dry white wine
1 tbsp. olive oil
pepper, salt

Time needed: 45 min.

Heat the oil and butter in a pan and add the finely sliced onions. Season with salt and pepper, cover and cook over low heat for about 30 minutes. Remove the lid, brown the onions slightly, douse with the white wine, letting it evaporate. Just before removing the onions from the heat sprinkle them with the chopped parsley.
Cook the spaghetti in a generous amount of salted boiling water and drain when "al dente", reserving 2 tablespoons of the cooking water. Toss with the onion sauce, add the 2 tablespoons of cooking water, sprinkle abundantly with the grated parmesan and serve straight away.

Spaghetti with aubergines *(serves 4)*

400 g (14 oz) spaghetti	1 small mozzarella cheese
	1 clove garlic
Sauce ingredients:	2 tbsp. grated parmesan
2 medium-sized aubergines	cheese
100 g (3½ oz) chicken breasts	1 small glass brandy
60 g (2¼ oz) butter	a little white flour
100 g (3½ oz) sliced boiled ham	olive oil
4 ripe tomatoes	freshly ground pepper
1 small onion	salt

Time needed: 1 hr.

Melt half the butter in a pan, add the finely chopped onion and the garlic clove crushed with a fork; add the diced chicken breasts and diced ham; blend the ingredients well, season with salt and pepper, douse with the brandy and let it evaporate.
Scald the tomatoes in boiling water, strain and skin them. Remove the seeds and cut the pulp into strips. Add to the other ingredients and cook for a further 10 minutes.
Wash, dry and slice the aubergines. Arrange them in layers on a plate, salt each layer and leave them for 30 minutes. Press them

in a colander to eliminate their rather bitter-tasting water-content, dry them and cut into strips; flour them and fry in plenty of oil.

Cook the spaghetti in salted boiling water, drain when "al dente", tip into a bowl, toss with the remaining butter, grated parmesan and the sauce. Stir well, then top with the aubergine strips, the diced mozzarella and serve immediately.

Spaghetti with cheese and pepper *(serves 4)*

400 g (14 oz) spaghetti

Sauce ingredients:
80 g (3 oz) grated pecorino

cheese
1 tbsp. pounded black pepper
salt

Time needed: 30 min.

Cook the spaghetti in a generous amount of salted boiling water; drain when slightly "al dente", tip into a bowl and toss with the pecorino and the pepper, adding 2 tablespoons of cooking water (otherwise it would result too dry).
Mix well and serve immediately.

Spaghetti with larks *(serves 4)*

300 g (10 oz) spaghetti

Sauce ingredients:
8 larks
80 g (3 oz) smoked streaky bacon
50 g (2 oz) fat Parma ham
50 g (2 oz) butter
20 g (1 oz) dried mushrooms

2 chicken livers
3 tbsp. grated parmesan cheese
1 small onion
1 carrot
½ stick celery
1 small glass brandy
a little meat stock
olive oil, pepper salt

Time needed: 2 hrs.

Pluck the larks; remove the innards (keeping the livers), wash the birds thoroughly and dry them.

Soak the mushrooms in warm water for at least 15 minutes. Finely chop the bacon, ham, carrot, onion and celery, tip into a pan and fry gently in a few tablespoons of olive oil. As the ingredients wilt, add the larks and brown them all over. Moisten them with a little meat stock and cook for about 20 minutes. Once the larks are well cooked, place them on a plate to drain, smear them with a little of their juice and keep them warm.

Add half the butter to the sauce left in the pan and add the mushrooms (rinsed in their water and well squeezed), the chicken and lark livers, and blend the ingredients over high heat. Season with salt and pepper, douse with the brandy and, once this has evaporated, sieve the sauce.

Cook the spaghetti in a generous amount of salted boiling water, drain when "al dente" and tip into a large bowl. Toss with the sauce, the remaining butter and the grated parmesan. Add the finishing touch by placing the larks on top. Serve straight away.

Spaghetti in squid sauce *(serves 4)*

400 g (14 oz) spaghetti

Sauce ingredients:
400 g (14 oz) squid
400 g (14 oz) tomato pulp
1 or 2 cloves garlic
2 tbsp. chopped parsley

1 tbsp. chopped onion
1 chilli pepper or plenty of
  chilli powder
100 ml (3 fl oz) dry white
  wine
3 tbsp. olive oil
salt

Time needed: 2 hrs.

Clean the squid by removing the bone (widen the hood and slip it out), the horny beak at the centre of the tentacles and the ink-sac; rinse under running water, tug sharply to detach the tentacles from the hood, squeeze the body to remove the entrails and scrape both parts with a knife. Slice the tentacles thinly and cut the body into rings.

Heat the oil in a pan, add half the parsley, the chopped garlic and onion and fry until golden; then add the squid, stir and add the wine. Purée the tomato pulp and pour into the mixture. Season with a whole chilli pepper or a generous sprinkle of chilli powder and salt. Continue to cook over moderate heat until the squid is tender (adding a little boiling water if necessary).

Cook the spaghetti in plenty of salted boiling water, drain when "al dente" and tip into a large bowl. Just before removing the sauce from the heat, top with the remaining parsley, then pour over the spaghetti, mix and serve.

Spaghetti with crab *(serves 4)*

400 g (14 oz) spaghetti	½ tbsp. tomato ketchup
	100 ml (3 fl oz) cooking
Sauce ingredients:	cream
200 g (7 oz) tinned crab	1 small glass brandy
1 jar mayonnaise	1 sachet saffron
a few pickled gherkins	salt

Time needed: 30 min.

Cook the spaghetti in a generous amount of salted boiling water, drain when "al dente" and pass swiftly under cold running water to cool; drain again and tip into a bowl.

Pour the mayonnaise into a basin, add the saffron (dissolved in a little cream), the brandy, the remaining cream and the gherkins (chopped into rounds). Crumble the crab meat, add to the mayonnaise, stir in the ketchup and mix well. Dress the spaghetti with the sauce, stir and serve.

Spaghetti with seafood baked in grease proof paper (p. 118)

Spaghetti gourmet style *(serves 4)*

400 g (14 oz) spaghetti

Sauce ingredients:
200 g (7 oz) pork loin
100 g (3½ oz) boletus mushrooms
100 g (3½ oz) turkey breast
50 g (2 oz) smoked streaky
  bacon

25 g (1 oz) butter
1 onion
a 250 g (9 oz) tin skinned
  tomatoes
4 tbsp. grated parmesan
  cheese
a little dry white wine
2 tbsp. sunflower oil
salt

Time needed: 2 hrs. 30 min.

Clean and thinly slice the mushrooms. Dice the pork loin, turkey breast and bacon. Sieve the tomatoes.

Heat the oil and butter in a casserole and gently fry the chopped onion; add the diced meat and bacon, brown gently, then add the tomato purée and cook the sauce for about 1 hour over moderate heat, stirring occasionally.

Marinate the mushrooms in a little white wine for 20 minutes, add them to the meat sauce and cook for a further 30 minutes.

Cook the spaghetti in a generous amount of salted boiling water, drain when "al dente", toss with the meat sauce, mushrooms and grated parmesan; stir and serve immediately.

Spaghetti with seafood baked in grease proof paper *(serves 4)*

400 g (14 oz) spaghetti

Sauce ingredients:
1 kg (2 lb) mixture
  of mussels and clams
300 g (10 oz) prawns and

baby squid
1 clove garlic
1 piece chilli pepper
1 glass dry white wine
5 tbsp. olive oil
salt

Time needed: 1 hr. (plus the time necessary to marinate the seafood in the herb and garlic dressing).

118

Clean and wash the seafood, prawns and baby squid thoroughly. Heat the mussels and clams in a frying-pan, douse them with white wine and, as the shells open, detach the molluscs and place them on a plate with the prawns and squid. Chop the garlic, parsley and hot pepper, and mix together with the oil; pour onto the seafood and leave for 2 hours, stirring occasionally, to make the flavours blend. Boil the spaghetti in a lot of salted water, drain when "al dente", tip into a bowl and toss with the seafood, prawns and squid. Wrap in a sheet of greaseproof paper or foil, rolling the edges firmly, and bake in a hot oven (200°C/400°F/Gas 6). When the wrapping appears "inflated", remove from the oven, place on a large serving dish, open at table and serve.

Spaghettini with curry sauce *(serves 4)*

400 g (14 oz) fine spaghetti	1 tbsp. hot curry powder
	½ bay leaf
Sauce ingredients:	chopped parsley and celery
70 g (2½ oz) butter	1 pinch thyme
100 g (3½ oz) sliced onion	1 fragment mace or a little
1 lemon	grated nutmeg
3 tbsp. white flour	400 ml (¾ pint) milk
200 ml (6 fl oz) cooking cream	freshly ground pepper, salt

Time needed: 30 min.

Boil the spaghetti in plenty of salted water. Meanwhile, prepare the sauce. Gently fry the chopped onion in the butter; as it turns slightly golden add the mixture of chopped parsley, celery, thyme, bay leaf and mace. Sieve in the flour, stir and add the curry powder. Blend all the ingredients well; cook slowly for several minutes, then add the broth, stir again, season and bring to the boil. Cook for about 40 minutes, then strain through a cloth, put back over the heat, bring to a simmer again and add the cream and a few drops of lemon juice. Drain the spaghetti when "al dente", tip into a warmed bowl, toss with the remaining butter (cut into knobs), and the curry sauce. Top with a dash of

freshly ground pepper, stir through and serve hot.

Curry sauce is also a success with ribbed pasta, vermicelli, linguine, bucatini and tagliatelle. Add an exotic touch by sieving half a banana into the finished sauce and garnishing the dish with slices of banana sautéed in butter.

Spaghettini with walnut sauce *(serves 4)*

400 g (14 oz) fine spaghetti

Sauce ingredients:
80 g (3 oz) walnut kernels
40 g (1½ oz) mascarpone
   cheese

80 g (3 oz) gorgonzola
   cheese
60 g (2¼ oz) butter
2 tbsp. grated parmesan
freshly ground pepper
salt

Time needed: 45 min.

Boil the spaghetti in plenty of salted water. In the meantime, prepare the walnut dressing. Finely chop half the walnut kernels, place in a bowl and add the sieved gorgonzola and the mascarpone. Add 45 g (1½ oz) of softened butter and blend the ingredients carefully into a smooth, creamy mixture. Now add the remaining walnuts, chopped coarsely. Drain the pasta when "al dente" and tip into a warmed bowl. Toss with the walnut sauce; melt and add the rest of the butter, the grated parmesan and a good sprinkle of freshly ground pepper. Stir well and serve.

Spaghettini served cold with raw peppers *(serves 4)*

400 g (14 oz) fine spaghetti

Sauce ingredients:
3 large, ripe tomatoes
1 red and 1 yellow pepper
1 small bunch basil

1 tbsp. mustard
a few drops of Worcester-
   shire sauce
6 tbsp. olive oil
1 lemon
salt

Time needed: 1 hr. 30 min.

Scald the tomatoes for a few moments in boiling water; drain and skin them, remove the seeds and cut them into strips. Cook the peppers over a flame. Rub off the burnt outer skin with a dry cloth, remove the seeds and fleshy white insides and dice. Beat the lemon juice and a pinch of salt in a cup; add the olive oil, the mustard and the Worcestershire sauce and mix well. Cook the pasta in a generous amount of salted boiling water; drain when "al dente" and pass briefly under cold running water, drain again and tip into a bowl. Toss with the peppers, the tomatoes and the sauce. Salt to taste, sprinkle with the chopped basil and keep in a cool place for at least 1 hour before serving.

Tagliatelle in cocoa sauce *(serves 4)*

400 g (14 oz) home-made egg tagliatelle

Sauce ingredients:
200 g (7 oz) ricotta cheese

50 g (2 oz) butter
50 g (2 oz) grated parmesan
1 tbsp. cocoa powder
1 pinch cinnamon powder
pepper, salt

Time needed: 30 min.

Boil the tagliatelle in plenty of salted water. Beat the ricotta in a basin and add the parmesan. Heat the creamy mixture in a metal colander over the pasta pan. Melt and brown the butter in a separate pan over moderate heat. Drain the tagliatelle and tip them into a serving bowl. Toss them with the melted butter, mix well and pour on the ricotta mixture. Sprinkle them with the cocoa and a pinch of cinnamon, add a dash of pepper and serve.

Tagliatelle with Parma ham *(serves 4)*

400 g (14 oz) home-made egg
  tagliatelle

Sauce ingredients:
500 g (1 lb) tinned skinned
  tomatoes

100 g (3½ oz) Parma
  ham
30 g (1 oz) butter
4 tbsp. olive oil
pepper
salt

Time needed: 30 min.

Put the tagliatelle on to cook in abundant salted boiling water, then prepare the sauce.
Coarsely chop the Parma ham and brown it gently in the butter.
Heat the oil in a casserole, add the mashed tomatoes, salt to taste and cook for a few minutes. Drain the tagliatelle, tip them into a bowl and toss with the tomato sauce. Top with the ham and its cooking juices and serve straight away.

Tagliatelle with ham and peas *(serves 4)*

400 g (14 oz) home-made egg
  tagliatelle

Sauce ingredients:
100 g (3½ oz) boiled ham
500 g (1 lb) fresh peas
80 g (3 oz) butter

100 g (3½ oz) grated parmesan
  cheese
1 tbsp. chopped fresh parsley
1 small onion
½ glass milk
1 pinch sugar
olive oil, salt, pepper

Time needed: 40 min.

Shell the peas and cut the ham into strips.
Melt half the butter, add the finely chopped onion and one tablespoon of water; cook but do not fry the onion. Tip the peas into the same pan, add the milk, a pinch of sugar, salt to taste and a little water (if necessary) to cover the peas. Cover and cook for about 30 minutes over low heat.

Cook the tagliatelle in salted boiling water, drain when "al dente" and pour into a large bowl. Dress the pasta with the hot pea sauce, the remaining butter (cut into knobs), half the boiled ham and the grated parmesan. Stir well, decorate the pasta with the rest of the ham and serve.

Tagliatelle with courgettes *(serves 4)*

400 g (14 oz) home-made egg
   tagliatelle

Dressing ingredients:
300 g (10 oz) courgettes
1 handful chopped parsley

1 clove garlic
50 g (2 oz) grated parmesan
   cheese
4 tbsp. olive oil
oregano
freshly ground pepper, salt

Time needed: 1 hr.

Top and tail, wash, dry and dice the courgettes. Heat the oil in a frying-pan with the crushed garlic clove, add the courgettes, fry, mixing frequently and, when they are cooked, sprinkle in a generous handful of finely chopped parsley and good pinches of oregano, salt and freshly ground pepper.
Cook the tagliatelle in plenty of boiling salted water, drain when "al dente" and tip them into the frying-pan with the courgettes. Blend well over the heat for a few minutes then serve piping hot.

Tagliatelle chef style *(serves 4)*

400 g (14 oz) home-made egg
   tagliatelle

Sauce ingredients:
one 150 g (5½ oz) slice smoked
   streaky bacon
one 50 g (2 oz) slice coppa

200 g (7 oz) tomato pulp
30 g (1 oz) butter
1 anchovy fillet
1 tbsp. finely chopped onion
1 clove garlic
100 g (3½ oz) grated parmesan
   cheese

Tagliatelle in cocoa sauce (p. 122)

a little dry white wine	olive oil
a little broth	pepper
a generous pinch of oregano	salt

Time needed: 45 min. (plus the time required to make the tagliatelle).

Dice the coppa and the bacon.

Finely chop the onion, crush the clove of garlic and fry in the butter and 2 tablespoons of olive oil, preferably using an earthenware casserole. As the onion wilts, remove the garlic, add the diced coppa and bacon and fry over high heat.

Douse with a little dry white wine and let it evaporate, then add the tomato pulp, the mashed anchovy fillet and 2 to 3 tablespoons of broth. Thicken the sauce and, just before removing it from the heat, taste, add salt if necessary, a dash of pepper and a generous pinch of oregano.

Cook the tagliatelle in plenty of boiling salted water, drain when "al dente" and toss with the sauce and grated parmesan.

Stir through and serve hot.

Tagliatelle verdi (Green tagliatelle) in cheese sauce *(serves 4)*

400 g (14 oz) home-made green tagliatelle	50 g (2 oz) Dutch cheese
	50 g (2 oz) provolone cheese
	1 small mozzarella cheese
Sauce ingredients:	70 g (2½ oz) butter
50 g (2 oz) gruyère cheese	freshly ground pepper, salt

Time needed: 40 min.

Using a pestle and mortar pound a few grains of pepper; slice the mozzarella thinly and cut the gruyère, Dutch cheese and provolone into narrow sticks.

Cook the tagliatelle in a generous amount of salted boiling water, drain when "al dente" (saving a ladle of the cooking water), and tip them into an ovenproof dish. Add the ladle of cooking water, the butter cut into pieces and the sticks of cheese; cover with the slices of mozzarella, season with pepper and bake in a hot oven pre-heated to 190°C/375°F/Gas 5 just until the cheese melts.

Taglierini with caviar *(serves 4)*

400 g (14 oz) home-made taglierini	(preferably German caviar)
	50 g (2 oz) butter
	cut into knobs
Sauce ingredients:	the juice of 1 lemon
2 tins of caviar	salt

Time needed: 20 min. (plus the time required to prepare the taglierini).

Begin to boil the taglierini in plenty of salted water. Squeeze the lemon juice over the caviar and cut the butter. Drain the taglierini when "al dente" (saving 2 tablespoons of their cooking water) and tip them into a warmed bowl. Add the 2 tablespoons of cooking water, the butter and the caviar, mix and serve at once.

Taglierini in cooked salame sauce *(serves 4)*

400 g (14 oz) home-made taglierini	1 tbsp. tomato paste
	$\frac{1}{2}$ onion
	1 clove garlic
Sauce ingredients:	1 sprig rosemary
70 g (2½ oz) minced cooked salame	$\frac{1}{2}$ glass red wine
	a few tablespoons broth
30 g (1 oz) butter	3 tbsp. olive oil
2 tbsp. grated parmesan cheese	pepper, salt

Time needed: 1 hr. (plus the time required to prepare the taglierini)

Heat the oil and butter in a pan and fry the chopped onion, the garlic and the rosemary. Add the cooked salame; stir, douse with the red wine, let it evaporate almost completely, then season, add the tomato paste diluted in a little hot broth and thicken the sauce over moderate heat. Cook the taglierini in plenty of salted boiling water, drain when "al dente" and tip into a bowl. Toss with the sauce and the parmesan, stir gently and serve.

Taglierini with agaric mushrooms *(serves 4)*

350 g (12½ oz) home-made egg taglierini

Sauce ingredients:
70 g (2½ oz) softened butter
70 g (2½ oz) diced boiled ham

4 agaric mushrooms (only half-open)
70 g (2½ oz) grated Swiss gruyère cheese
2 tbsp. cooking cream
pepper, salt

Time needed: 25 min.

Cook the taglierini in plenty of salted boiling water and drain just "al dente". Clean the mushrooms, leaving them whole.
Beat the butter in a bowl, using a wooden spoon, until it becomes soft and creamy. Tip the taglierini into the bowl, add the cream, the diced ham and the grated gruyère. Arrange all the ingredients in an ovenproof dish, sprinkle generously with freshly ground pepper and cover the pasta with the mushrooms cut into slivers (using a truffle-slicer, if you have one). Bake in a hot oven (200°C/400°F/Gas 6) for 5 minutes, and serve in the same dish.

Timballo with rigatoni *(serves 4)*

350 g (12½ oz) rigatoni

Sauce ingredients:
300 g (10 oz) spinach
150 g (5½ oz) butter

80 g (3 oz) grated parmesan
½ litre (1 pint) milk
2 tbsp. white flour
1 pinch nutmeg
salt

Time needed: 1 hr.

Trim, wash and boil the spinach, stirring it with a wooden spoon in a saucepan over moderate heat, using only the water left on the leaves after washing. Drain, squeeze, chop and cook the spinach gently in 25 g (1 oz) of melted butter and a pinch of salt.

Boil the milk and prepare the béchamel by melting 50 g (2 oz) butter in a casserole, sieving in the flour, mixing well with a wooden spoon to crush any lumps and adding the boiling milk, a little at a time.

Cook the sauce for 5 minutes, stirring continuously; remove from the heat and season with salt and a dash of nutmeg.

Cook the rigatoni in an abundant quantity of boiling salted water, drain when well cooked and tip them into a bowl. Add the spinach, the remaining butter cut into knobs, (save one piece), and the 2 tablespoons of grated parmesan.

Grease a timbale mould, tip in the pasta, sprinkle with the rest of the grated parmesan, add a few slivers of butter and steam (using a bain-marie) in a hot oven pre-heated to 190°C/375°F/Gas 5 for about 15 minutes. Take it out of the oven, leave it to cool for about 10 minutes, then turn it onto a plate and serve.

Torciglioni alla ciociara (from Ciociaria, in the Roman countryside) *(serves 4)*

400 g (14 oz) torciglioni	80 g (3 oz) grated pecorino cheese
Sauce ingredients:	6 tbsp. olive oil
500 g (1 lb) ripe tomatoes	1 sprig fresh oregano
150 g (5½ oz) mozzarella cheese	freshly ground pepper
	salt

Time needed: 50 min.

Wash, dry and cut the tomatoes into pieces, removing the seeds. Heat 2 to 3 tablespoons of oil in an earthenware casserole, add the tomatoes and the diced mozzarella and stir with a wooden spoon until the mozzarella melts and turns "stringy". Then add the pecorino, season with salt, pepper and the crumbled oregano. Cover and cook over high heat for 15 minutes, stirring frequently. Meanwhile, cook the torciglioni in plenty of boiling salted water, drain when "al dente" and toss with the sauce. Tip into a lightly greased ovenproof dish and brown in a hot oven pre-heated to 190°C/375°F/Gas 5. Serve hot.

Tortelli "with a tail" *(serves 4)*

Pasta ingredients:
a sheet of dough made from
   400 g (14 oz) white flour
   and 4 eggs

Filling ingredients:
1 kg (2 lb) spinach
250 g (9 oz) ricotta cheese
50 g (2 oz) mascarpone cheese
4 tbsp. grated parmesan cheese
1 egg

freshly ground pepper
salt

Sauce ingredients:
home-made tomato sauce
   with basil (or strained
   skinned, pulped tinned
   tomatoes and chopped basil)
70 g (2½ oz) butter
3 tbsp. grated parmesan cheese
salt

Time needed: 2 hrs.

To make the filling, boil, drain, squeeze dry and chop the spinach finely. Mix it in a bowl with the sieved ricotta, the mascarpone, the parmesan, the egg, and the salt and pepper, until the mixture is creamy. Place small heaps of filling 8-9 cm (3-3½ inches) apart on the sheet of dough; fold the edge of the pasta over to cover them and cut off the strip of filled pasta with a cutting-wheel. Press firmly all around each mound of filling and use the cutting-wheel to divide the strip into rectangles. Hold each rectangle firmly by the ends and twist as though wrapping a sweet. Cook the tortelli in plenty of salted boiling water and heat up the tomato sauce. Drain the pasta gently, using a skimmer, and dress in a bowl with the melted butter and the parmesan. Serve the hot tomato sauce separately.

Tortelli with potatoes and onions *(serves 4)*

Pasta ingredients:
a sheet of dough made from
400 g (14 oz) white flour and
4 eggs

Filling ingredients:
500 g (1 lb) potatoes
70 g (2½ oz) minced bacon
2 medium-sized onions
2 tbsp. grated parmesan cheese

1 egg-yolk
2 tbsp. olive oil
1 tbsp. parsley chopped with
½ clove garlic
pepper, salt

Dressing ingredients:
80 g (3 oz) butter
2 tbsp. grated parmesan cheese
salt

Time needed: 2 hrs.

To make the filling, chop the onion finely and fry gently with
the oil and the bacon over low heat. Boil, peel and mash the
potatoes; mix them in a bowl together with the onions, bacon,
chopped parsley and garlic, parmesan, egg-yolk and pinches of
salt and pepper.
Using a round, serrated, 5 cm (2 inch)-diameter pastry-cutter, cut
out discs of dough; place blobs of filling on half of them and use
the other half as covers. Press firmly round the edges to seal well
and leave the tortelli to rest a while. Boil them in plenty of salted
water, drain and dress them in layers with slightly browned
melted butter and sprinklings of parmesan. Serve at once.

Tortellini alla bolognese (Bologna style) *(serves 4)*

Pasta ingredients:
a sheet of dough made from
400 g (14 oz) white flour
and 4 eggs

Filling ingredients:
150 g (5½ oz) pork loin
150 g (5½ oz) turkey or

chicken breast
80 g (3 oz) Bologna sausage
100 g (3½ oz) Parma ham
1 egg
150 g (5½ oz) grated parmesan
cheese
25 g (1 oz) butter
nutmeg, pepper, salt

*Torciglioni alla ciociara (p. 130) and Tortelli
"with a tail" (p. 131)*

Sauce ingredients:
80 g (3 oz) grated parmesan
   cheese

an excellent ragù (meat
   sauce) or tomato sauce (see
   "Ravioli with ragù" p. 99)

Time needed: 2 hrs.

Melt the butter in a pan, add the cut up pork and turkey (or
chicken) breast, and brown over moderate heat for about 10
minutes.

Mince with the ham and sausage; add the egg, parmesan,
pinches of salt, pepper and nutmeg and stir to a smooth,
well-mixed paste.

Use the dough and the filling to prepare tortellini as described
on p. 14. Cook the tortellini in a generous amount of salted
boiling water, drain and dress them with the meat or tomato
sauce and grated parmesan.

Tortelloni au gratin *(serves 4)*

Pasta ingredients:
a sheet of dough made from
   400 g (14 oz) white flour
   4 eggs
   and 200 g (7 oz) spinach
   (boiled and squeezed dry)

Filling ingredients:
350 g (12½ oz) fresh ricotta
   cheese
500 g (1 lb) boiled spinach
40 g (1½ oz) grated parmesan
   cheese
100 g (3½ oz) boiled ham
1 egg-yolk
a pinch of nutmeg

pepper
salt

Sauce ingredients:
400 g (14 oz) tomato pulp
50 g (2 oz) butter
40 g (1½ oz) grated parmesan
   cheese
1 sliced mozzarella cheese
1 small onion
a few leaves fresh
   basil (or ½ tbsp.
   dried basil)
olive oil
pepper
salt

Time needed: 2 hrs.

Prepare home-made green pasta by kneading the flour with the eggs and puréed spinach. Roll it into a thin sheet of dough.

Make the filling by mixing the chopped spinach and minced ham with the sieved ricotta, adding the parmesan, egg-yolk and a pinch of nutmeg, salt and pepper.

Cut the dough into 5-6 cm (2-2½ inch) squares with a punch or serrated pasta-wheel.

Drop a blob of filling on each, then fold over, joining the two opposite corners to form a triangle. Press firmly around the edges of each triangle and give them the shape of a bonnet by overlapping and pressing the two opposite points.

Prepare the sauce separately. Finely chop the onion and fry gently in 2 tablespoons of olive oil. Add the sieved tomato pulp, the basil, a pinch of salt and pepper and thicken the sauce over moderate heat, stirring now and again.

Cook the tortelloni in a generous amount of salted boiling water, drain when "al dente", toss in melted butter and arrange in layers in an ovenproof dish, dressing each layer with a sprinkle of parmesan and a little tomato sauce. Top with the sliced mozzarella and a final sprinkle of grated parmesan, then brown in a hot oven pre-heated to 200°C/400°F/Gas 6. Serve at once.

Trenette with clam sauce *(serves 4)*

400 g (14 oz) trenette

Sauce ingredients:
1 kg (2 lb) clams
250 g (9 oz) tinned, skinned tomatoes

1 tbsp. finely chopped parsley
2 cloves garlic
olive oil
pepper
salt

Time needed: 1 hr. 30 min.

Brush the clams vigorously under running water using a stiff brush and wash them well to eliminate any sand.

Heat a little oil in a pan and brown the garlic; add the clams and leave them over the heat until they open. Detach the molluscs from their shells and keep them warm.

Filter the liquid left in the pan and place back over the heat adding the sieved tomatoes, salt and pepper to taste. Thicken over moderate heat, stirring occasionally.

Cook the pasta in a generous amount of salted boiling water, drain when "al dente" and dress with the tomato sauce. Top with the clams, sprinkle with chopped parsley and serve.

Trenette Bari style *(serves 4)*

400 g (14 oz) trenette

Sauce ingredients:
150 g (5½ oz) minced pork loin
250 g (9 oz) tinned skinned tomatoes

¼ onion
1 stick celery
½ carrot
1 glass dry white wine
olive oil
pepper
salt

Time needed: 1 hr.

Heat half a glass of olive oil in a casserole and wilt the finely chopped onion, carrot and celery.

Add the minced pork, brown gently, then douse with a small glass of white wine; let it evaporate, then add the skinned tomatoes, season well with salt and pepper, cover and thicken over moderate heat.

Cook the trenette in a generous amount of salted boiling water, drain when "al dente", dress with the sauce, stir through and serve at once.

Trenette with clam sauce (p. 135)

Trofie with pesto *(serves 4)*

Pasta ingredients:
350 g (12½ oz) white flour
50 g (2 oz) bran

Pesto ingredients:
2 generous handfuls fresh
basil leaves
1 clove garlic

a generous handful pine
kernels
1 tbsp. Sardinian pecorino
cheese (not too strong)
1 tbsp. grated parmesan
cheese
1 glass olive oil
salt

Time needed: 1 hr. 30 min.

Trofie with pesto is a typically Ligurian dish, especially of the eastern Riviera.

To make the pasta, heap the flour and bran on the pastry-board, make a "crater" and add enough water, a drop at a time, to make a fairly stiff dough. Knead well, then cut up the dough and roll each piece into a long, thin sausage. Chop each "sausage" into thimble-sized pieces. Roll each piece of pasta obliquely across the prongs of a fork, rather like when making potato gnocchi.

To prepare the pesto, wash the basil leaves, lay them on a tea-towel to dry, then put them into a mortar with the garlic clove, pine kernels and a pinch of salt. Pound the leaves with the pestle against the bottom and sides of the mortar until all the ingredients are reduced to a pulp; amalgamate a little oil at a time and, lastly, grate the two cheeses, mix them together and add them to the mixture.

Cook the trofie in plenty of boiling salted water, drain and dress them generously with the pesto and serve at once.

Vermicelli al verde (with green sauce) *(serves 4)*

400 g (14 oz) vermicelli

Sauce ingredients:
200 g (7 oz) boiled spinach
1 tbsp. pine kernels
4 anchovy fillets

2 cloves garlic
1 small handful parsley
1 bunch fresh basil
5 tbsp. olive oil
pepper
salt

Time needed: 45 min.

Cook the vermicelli in a generous amount of salted boiling water. Make the sauce while the pasta is cooking by finely chopping the anchovy fillets, the cloves of garlic, parsley, basil leaves and spinach (squeezed dry).
Heat the oil in a casserole, add the chopped ingredients and the pine kernels and fry gently over moderate heat.
Drain the vermicelli when slightly "al dente" and arrange them in a greased ovenproof dish; dress them with the sauce and a good sprinkle of pepper and cook for a further 10 to 15 minutes in a hot oven (190°C/375°F/Gas 5). Serve hot in the same ovenproof dish.

Zite with pork ragù *(serves 4)*

400 g (14 oz) zite

Sauce ingredients:
250 g (9 oz) lean, minced pork
one 50 g (2 oz) slice smoked streaky bacon

250 g (9 oz) tinned skinned tomatoes
1 onion
1 tbsp. finely chopped parsley and basil
1 glass full-bodied red wine
olive oil, salt

Time needed: 2 hrs.

Finely chop the onion and carrot and dice the bacon.
Heat a little oil in a casserole and fry the diced bacon gently for

a few minutes, then add the chopped vegetables and the herbs and cook them until they wilt.

Add the minced pork, salt, and as the meat begins to turn golden douse the mixture with the red wine and let it evaporate.

Sieve the tomatoes and add to the mixture; cover and cook the ragù over very low heat, stirring from time to time and adding a drop of boiling water (or broth) if necessary.

In the meantime cook the pasta in a generous amount of salted boiling water, drain when "al dente", pour into a bowl and dress with the ragù. Stir well, possibly adding a dash of freshly ground pepper, and serve.

Zite with tuna sauce *(serves 4)*

400 g (14 oz) zite

Sauce ingredients:
500 g (1 lb) tomato pulp
50 g (2 oz) tuna fish in oil
50 g (2 oz) grated
   caciocavallo cheese

4 anchovy fillets
1 clove garlic
1 small onion
a pinch oregano
olive oil
salt
pepper

Time needed: 40 min.

Finely chop the garlic and onion; heat a few tablespoons of oil in a casserole and fry them gently; add the mashed anchovy fillets and the tomato pulp, cut into strips; season with salt, pepper and a pinch of oregano, and cook over moderate heat for about 20 minutes.

Meanwhile, cook the zite in a generous amount of salted boiling water and drain when "al dente".

Chop the tuna coarsely, add to the sauce and toss with the pasta in a bowl. Sprinkle generously with the grated cheese and serve immediately.

Trofie with pesto (p. 138)

INDEX OF RECIPES